GREAT
BATTLES
THROUGH
THE AGES

ROUTES OF THE
CRUSADERS

THE THIRD CRUSADE:

RICHARD THE LIONHEARTED vs. SALADIN

SAMUEL WILLARD CROMPTON

INTRODUCTION BY
CASPAR W. WEINBERGER

CHELSEA HOUSE
P U B L I S H E R S
A Haights Cross Communications Company
Philadelphia

FRONTIS: This map traces the routes of the Crusaders as they left Europe and set out on their way to battle the Muslims in the Holy Land of the Middle East.

CHELSEA HOUSE PUBLISHERS

VP, PRODUCT DEVELOPMENT Sally Cheney
DIRECTOR OF PRODUCTION Kim Shinners
CREATIVE MANAGER Takeshi Takahashi
MANUFACTURING MANAGER Diann Grasse

STAFF FOR THE THIRD CRUSADE: RICHARD THE LIONHEARTED VS. SALADIN

EXECUTIVE EDITOR Lee Marcott
SENIOR EDITOR Tara Koellhoffer
PRODUCTION ASSISTANT Megan Emery
PICTURE RESEARCHER Noelle Nardone
SERIES & COVER DESIGNER Takeshi Takahashi
LAYOUT 21st Century Publishing and Communications, Inc.

A Haights Cross Communications ⟍ Company

http://www.chelseahouse.com

First Printing

1 3 5 7 9 8 6 4 2

Library of Congress Cataloging-in-Publication Data

Crompton, Samuel Willard.
   The Third Crusade : Richard the Lionhearted vs. Saladin / Samuel Willard
Crompton.
     p. cm. -- (Great battles through the ages)
   ISBN 0-7910-7437-4
  1. Richard I, King of England, 1157-1199--Juvenile literature. 2. Saladin,
Sultan of Egypt and Syria, 1137-1193--Juvenile literature. 3. Crusades--Third,
1189-1192--Juvenile literature. I. Title. II. Series.
D163.C76 2003
956'.014--dc21

                                                                      2003004593

TABLE OF CONTENTS

INTRODUCTION

by Caspar W. Weinberger

There are many ways to study and teach history, which has perhaps been best defined as the "recording and interpretation of past events." Concentration can be on a compilation of major events, or on those events that help prove a theory of the author's. Or the "great man" theory can be applied to write the history of a country or an era, based on a study of the principal leaders or accepted geniuses who are felt to have shaped events that became part of the tapestry of history.

This new Chelsea House series adopts and continues the plan of studying six of the major battles and turning points of wars that did indeed shape much of the history of the periods before, during, and after those wars. By studying the events leading up to major battles and their results, inescapably one learns a great deal about the history of that period.

The first battle, chosen appropriately enough, is the Battle of Actium. There, in 31 B.C., the naval forces of Antony and Cleopatra, and those of Octavian, did battle off the northwest coast of Greece for control of the Roman world. Octavian's victory ended the Roman civil war and gave him unchallenged supremacy, leading to his designation as Augustus, Rome's first emperor. It is highly appropriate that the Battle of Actium be studied first for this series, because the battle was for many decades used as the starting point for a new era.

Next, in chronological order, is a study of the long years of battles between the forces of Richard the Lionhearted and Saladin. This Third Crusade, during the twelfth century, and the various military struggles for Acre and Jerusalem, was the background against which much of the history of modern Britain and Europe and the Middle East was played out.

Coming down to modern times, the series includes a study of the battle that forever changed naval warfare. This battle, the first between two ironclad warships, the *Monitor* and the *Merrimack*, ended the era of naval wars fought by great fleets of sail- or oar-powered ships, with their highly intricate maneuvers. After the *Monitor* and *Merrimack*, all naval battles became floating artillery duels with wholly different tactics and skills required.

The sinking of the German ship *Bismarck* during World War II was not so much a battle as a clear demonstration of the fact that a huge preponderance of naval force on one side could hunt down and destroy one of the most powerful battleships then afloat.

The continued importance of infantry warfare was demonstrated in the Battle of the Bulge, the final attempt of the German army, near the end of World War II, to stave off what in hindsight is now seen as the inevitable victory of the Allies.

The last battle in this series covers the Korean War—one of the most difficult and costly we have fought, and yet a war whose full story is very nearly forgotten by historians and teachers. The story of the Korean War embodies far more than simply the history of a war we fought in the 1950s. It is a history that is dominated by General Douglas MacArthur—but it is also a history of many of the foundation stores of American foreign and domestic policy in the past half century.

These six battles, and the wars of which they were a part, are well worth studying because, although they obviously cannot recount all of history from Actium to Korea, they can and do show the reader the similarities of many of those issues that drive people and governments to war. They also recount the development and changes in technologies by which people have acquired the ability to destroy their fellow creatures ever more effectively and completely.

With the invention and deployment of each new instrument of destruction, from the catapults that were capable of blasting great holes in the walls defending castles and forts, to today's nuclear weapons, the prediction has always been made that the effects and capability of each of those engines of destruction were so awful that their very availability would end war entirely. Thus far, those predictions have always been wrong, although as the full potential of nuclear weapons of mass destruction is increasingly better understood, it may well be that the very nature of these ultimate weapons will, indeed, mean that they will ever be used. However, the sheer numbers of these ultimate weapons possessed by many countries, and the possibilities of some of those countries falling under the dictatorship of some of the world's most dangerous leaders, combine to make imaginable a war that could indeed end the world. That is why the United States has expended so much to try to prevent countries such as Iraq and North Korea from continuing to be led by men as inherently dangerous as Saddam Hussein and Kim Sung Il, who are determined to acquire the world's most dangerous weapons.

An increasing knowledge of some of the great battles of the past that have so influenced history is essential unless we want to fulfill the old adage that those who forget history are likely to be condemned to repeat it—with all of its mistakes.

This old adage reminds us also that history is a study not just of great military victories, but also the story of battles lost and the many mistakes that were made by even the greatest of commanders.

After every engagement that involves American troops in action, even on a very small scale, the Pentagon conducts a "Lessons Learned" exercise. What went wrong? What should have been done differently? Did we need more troops, more artillery, more planes? Most important, could more lives of our own troops have been saved?

These mistakes or command errors are not only carefully studied and written about, but they form the basis for war games or exercises in which actual battle situations are re-fought— sometimes on paper—but frequently with troops re-enacting various parts of the combat action. These "lessons learned" exercises become a valuable part of the training of troops and are an even more valuable part of the training of leaders and commanders.

As we can all guess from the short discussions of some of those great battles in this series, there were many opportunities for different commanders and different plans to be used. Indeed, history is perhaps our greatest teacher, and a study of great battles is a great way to learn, even though each battle is different and there will be different lessons to be learned from the post-battle studies.

So, this Chelsea House series serves as a splendid beginning to our study of military history—a history that we must master if we want to see the expansion and success of our basic policy of maintaining peace with freedom.

It is not enough to consider threats to our security and our freedom. We must also be constantly ready to defend our freedom by keeping our ability to prevent any of those threats against us from materializing into real dangers. The study of great battles and how they were won, despite mistakes that have been made, is a vital part of our ability to keep peace with freedom.

BY: Caspar W. Weinberger
Chairman, FORBES Inc.
March 2003

Caspar W. Weinberger was the fifteenth U.S. secretary of defense, serving under President Ronald Reagan from 1981 to 1987.

The First Crusade began in 1095, with a speech by Pope Urban II. The Crusaders reached and conquered Jerusalem in 1099. Christian Europe now had become a military force to be feared.

The First Crusade

Deus Volt! (God wills it!)

—Shouts of French knights on hearing
the speech of Pope Urban II

In the autumn of 1095, Pope Urban II went to Clermont, in south-central France. Perhaps as many as 10,000 people, many of them knights, gathered to hear the pope speak. Those in the audience knew that this was an important day, a historic moment. Pope Urban did not leave Italy very often, and he seldom addressed such a large crowd of people outdoors.

All the chroniclers agree that the pope gave a masterful speech. He recalled that a new group of infidels (non-Christians) had recently taken over the Holy Land, and that they were preventing Christian pilgrims from visiting sites where Jesus Christ had lived. The pope referred to the so-called infidels as a "new accursed race of Persians," but they were in fact Seljuk Turks, who had migrated to the Middle East from Central Asia and adopted the Muslim faith.

Pope Urban went on to explain how he thought that Europe—and France in particular—was overpopulated. He pointed out that many of the fights between knights and lords were caused by this overpopulation. Then he described Jerusalem and the Holy Land as the center of the world, pleasant and beautiful. Toward the end of his speech, Pope Urban called on the knights and warriors of Christian Europe to go forth on a great crusade to free the Holy Land from the infidels. The knights in attendance took up the battle cry, "Deus Volt (God wills it!)"[1] Thus was born the First Crusade.

Jerusalem had been in Arab or Turkish hands for more than 400 years. Even so, during most of that time, the rulers had allowed Christian pilgrims to visit the city. Now the Seljuk Turks, who represented a new, more militant sect of Islam, denied Christians visitation rights.

The pope's speech inspired men and women all across Europe. The knights of France began at once to collect arms and money for the great crusade to the east. Even as they gathered horses and armor, however, another group, self-appointed, started on its way to the Holy Land. The two groups would actually represent different sectors of the same crusade. They were known as the Peasants' Crusade and the Knights' Crusade.

The peasants, the self-appointed Crusaders, were ready to go long before the knights. Led by a self-ordained preacher named Peter the Hermit, about 30,000 members of the European peasant class began the long march to the east in 1096. Along the way they attacked Jewish communities in and around Strasbourg, France; the Crusaders saw harassing the Jews as part of their holy mission to free Jerusalem.

In the summer of 1096, the peasant Crusaders arrived at the great and beautiful city of Constantinople, center of the Byzantine Empire, located where Europe and Asia meet. Byzantine Emperor Alexius was concerned by the appearance and attitude of the Crusaders; he had them quickly ferried across the Straits of the Bosporus into what is now Turkey.

Peter the Hermit and his 30,000 followers blundered into the mountainous areas of western Turkey. There, just about 100 miles (161 kilometers) east of Constantinople, they were ambushed and almost wiped out by an army of Turks. Peter and a small group of survivors lived to return to Europe to tell their tale of the awful mountain terrain and an implacable foe, the Seljuk Turks.

Later in the year 1096, the Knights' Crusade set out from France. The knights followed almost exactly the same route that the peasants had taken, and after many months of arduous struggle, they, too, reached the gates of Constantinople. If Emperor Alexius had been confused or angered by the peasants, he was bewildered and frightened by the appearance of the knights. Alexius made all the leaders of the Knights' Crusade swear an oath of allegiance to him, so that any and all lands they might conquer in the Holy Land would come under his rule. Then Alexius had the Crusaders ferried across the Bosporus.

The knights were better armed and better led than the peasants who had gone before them. Even though the Turks made some attacks in the mountain passes, the

The Peasants' Crusade, led by Peter the Hermit, set out in 1096. The peasants fought among themselves along the way, and attacked communities of Jews on their march.

knights made their way across Turkey, through what are called the Cilician Gates, and onto the open plains near the northeast corner of the Mediterranean Sea. There, the knights came upon the city of Antioch on the Orontes River.

Antioch was one of the oldest and most prosperous cities anywhere on the Mediterranean. It had thrived during Roman times, and was still a center for trade and commerce. The Crusader knights captured and occupied the city, only to find themselves quickly besieged by a much larger army of Seljuk Turks, many of whom had come from as far away as Baghdad and Mosul, in what is now Iraq.

The Crusaders were soon in a state of despair. They had enough food and water to hold out for a long time, but it seemed inevitable that they would eventually be soundly defeated by the great army situated on the plain outside Antioch. Then, a humble member of the crusade came forward to tell the others about a dream he had had.

The night before, he had dreamed that the Holy Lance—the one that had pierced Jesus Christ's side as he hung on the cross—was in the city of Antioch. He begged permission to be allowed to find the Holy Lance. Not only was permission granted, but about half of the Christian army spent the day searching for the lance. Sometime around sundown, a lance was found and brought forward. The Crusaders believed it was, indeed, the Holy Lance.

Inspired by the find, the leaders of the crusading army decided to go forth the next day and meet the Turks on the open plain below the city. This seemed to be madness, but the Crusaders were both desperate and inspired by their discovery of the lance.

The battle the next day was one-sided. The Crusaders won a great victory, and the Turkish army scattered. The way was open for the Crusaders to proceed south, on their way to the holy city of Jerusalem.

The Crusaders continued down the Mediterranean coast, and in June 1099, they came to the walls of Jerusalem. The Turkish defenders had poisoned all the

Middle Eastern Trade

In reading the story of the Crusades, one might think that nothing but war took place in the Middle East. This was not the case; the exchange of goods and materials was a vital element in Middle Eastern life.

Within one generation of their conquest of the Holy Land, the European Crusaders found much in the Middle East that was to their liking. Spices such as jasmine, oranges and other fruits, and Arab innovations such as the lateen-rigged sail (a special triangular sail used often in the Mediterranean) all became regular parts of the lives of the Christian Crusaders. Those goods and inventions also found their way to Europe.

Venice, Genoa, and Pisa—three Italian cities—provided the ships and sailors that brought goods back and forth across the Mediterranean Sea. All three cities profited from the trade with the Middle East, which they called *Outremer*, meaning "land beyond the sea." Arab and Turkish luxury goods found their way to Italy, and then across the Alps into Northern Europe.

There were many port cities along the coast of the Holy Land, many of which became battle sites during the Third Crusade. The two largest cities, though, and the ones that benefited most from trade between Arabs and Christians, were Constantinople, the capital of the Byzantine Empire, and Cairo, capital of Arab Egypt.

Throughout Greek and Roman times, Alexandria, located at the mouth of the Nile River, had been the center of Egyptian commerce. Now it was surpassed by Cairo. Gold, silver, spices, and fruits all found their way to the narrow street markets of Cairo, and the wealth of the Egyptian sultan (ruler) increased accordingly.

wells within a ten-mile (16-kilometer) vicinity, but this did not daunt the Crusaders. They spent three days in prayer and silent marches around the city, because they believed they had to purify themselves in order to enter Jerusalem. After making these preparations, they commenced their attack.

It took about three days, but the Crusaders broke

This map shows the sea route from Venice to Constantinople. The Venetians and Byzantines were trade rivals. Later, in 1204, the Venetian would persuade the leaders of the Fourth Crusade to attack and sack Constantinople. Important relics of Byzantine art are still in Venice today.

In fact, one of the reasons the Muslims began the *jihad* (holy war) of 1187 was to prevent Christians in the Holy Land from intercepting Muslim caravans between Cairo and Damascus, in present-day Syria.

through Jerusalem's gates and walls. They entered the Holy City that Pope Urban had urged them to seize some four years earlier. They proceeded to murder almost everyone they found: Turks, Arabs, and Jews alike. The massacre was horrendous. Thousands upon thousands of civilians were slaughtered by Christian knights who had sworn to defend the innocent and helpless.

Pope Urban II died shortly before the news arrived that Jerusalem had been taken. His successor, Paschal II, and the other Christian leaders of Europe, worked to make sure that the Holy Land remained in Christian hands.

The Holy Land was divided into four principalities: the Kingdom of Jerusalem, the County of Edessa, the Principality of Antioch, and the County of Tripoli. Each of these four states was ruled by a European knight or lord. The victorious Crusaders also built magnificent castles throughout the Holy Land, in order to assure their continued dominance. The most remarkable of the castles was—and is—the Krak de Chevaliers ("Castle of the Knights"). Built on a summit overlooking a river valley, the Krak de Chevaliers remains a major tourist site in Syria to this day.

After the Christians took over the Holy Land, two groups of knights formed in order to help protect it. The Knights Templar took vows as monks, becoming what were called "Warrior Monks." They made it their duty to ensure the safety of pilgrims as they traveled to the Holy Land. The other order of knights was the Hospitallers, who devoted themselves to the care of the sick and the poor in the Holy Land.

Two generations passed. During that time, many of the Crusaders and their descendants grew to love the

Holy Land for its climate and riches as well as its sacred sites. Many of the Crusaders learned to dress as the Arabs and Turks did, in flowing robes. A large number of them also became prominent merchants who dealt in spices, silk, and other luxury goods. In short, the Christians thrived in the land that they had conquered.

This anonymous portrait of Saladin hangs in the Museo di Andrea del Castagno in Uffizi, Italy. Saladin was not an Arab, but rather a Kurd. Still, he became the best known and best loved of all Muslim leaders of his era.

The Second Crusade and the *Jihad* of 1187

Vengeance for Islam! God is mighty!
God conquers and subdues! He humbleth the infidel!

— Sermon of Muhi ad-Din in 1187

For the first two generations after the conquest, the Christians in the Holy Land had little fear of the Arabs or Turks. The Muslims were in disarray, fighting among themselves. Then, however, the Arab world found two new leaders: Zengi and Nur ad-Din.

Zengi was a Kurd, rather than an Arab or Turk. The Kurds were a prominent ethnic minority in the Middle East; they remain today one of the largest ethnic groups that does not have its own political state.

21

Zengi created a fierce new Arab-Turkish army, and in December 1146, he captured Edessa, one of the Crusader states. Both the loss of the city and its timing alarmed Christian Europeans. The news spread rapidly, and in March 1147, a monk named Bernard of Clairvaux preached in support of a second crusade. He gave his speech in southern France, and, like Pope Urban II's 1095 address, it was a great success.

German and French soldiers made up the bulk of the Christian army. King Louis VII of France and his wife, Eleanor of Aquitaine, went together on the crusade. Conrad III, the Holy Roman emperor, led the German forces. He was accompanied by his nephew, who would later succeed him as Emperor Frederick Barbarossa. They had hardly reached Constantinople when they learned that the German branch of the army had been nearly destroyed in the mountains of Turkey. Although Louis VII and Eleanor continued on their journey, making it all the way to Jerusalem, they never managed to retake Edessa. One of the four Christian principalities was gone, and the Second Crusade had been a dismal failure.

The situation was not perfect for the Muslims, either. Zengi was assassinated by a disgruntled servant in 1147. He was succeeded by his son, Nur ad-Din, who worked to unify the Arabs and Turks in Mesopotamia, which is Iraq today. Nur ad-Din wanted to bring both Syria and Egypt under Muslim control; in doing so, he would place Muslim forces on both sides of the Christians who occupied the Holy Land. It took a number of years, but Nur ad-Din was able to conquer all of Syria. He made Damascus his capital, and sent one of his principal lieutenants to seize Egypt. This lieutenant was named Saladin.

Saladin's full name was Yusuf ibn Ayyub Salad ad-Din, which means "Bounty of Faith." Born in 1137 in what is now Iraq, Saladin was a Kurd. He had essentially been adopted by Nur ad-Din, the leader of Muslim Damascus. Saladin developed strong diplomatic and military skills, and by about 1172, he was master of the Muslim province of Egypt and the province of Syria, centered at Damascus. Because of his increasing power, Nur ad-Din felt betrayed by Saladin. The two Kurdish leaders might have come to blows had not the elder of the two died unexpectedly in 1174. Saladin soon imposed his rule on Damascus as well as Egypt. Despite their disagreements, Saladin had become Nur ad-Din's heir.

Lying between Damascus, Syria, and Cairo, Egypt, were the Christian kingdoms that had been founded after the successful First Crusade, between 1095 and 1099. By 1174, the relationship between the Christian Crusaders and the Muslim inhabitants was simultaneously profitable and strained. Both the Muslims and Christians benefited from the trade between them, but neither group was pleased about the continued presence of the other in the Holy Land.

Baldwin the Leper, king of Jerusalem, died in 1185. His replacement was Guy of Lusignan, who was chosen as part of a compromise by the nobles of the kingdom. Guy lacked authority as he began his reign, and therefore, he catered to some of the nobles whose support he needed. One of these people was Reginald of Châtillon.

Reginald had a vendetta against his Muslim neighbors. In 1185, he sponsored an expedition against the holy cities of Mecca and Medina, both of which are now in Saudi Arabia. Although the expedition was thwarted by a swift movement of Muslim troops, Saladin still developed a bitter hatred of Reginald and his virulent anti-Muslim beliefs.

In 1186, Reginald went even further; he stopped a Muslim merchant caravan and took its members as prisoners to the Krak de Chevaliers. Among the captives was one

Les Krak des Chevaliers was, and is, a stupendous work of military engineering. The Knights Hospitaller finished the construction in 1131. From this castle, the Christian knights could observe the movements of their enemies for many miles in all directions.

of Saladin's sisters. When the Muslim leader petitioned for his sister's release, he received the insolent response, "Let Allah come and free her."

In March 1187, Saladin had announced his own holy war, which the Muslims called *jihad*. This is a kind of war that is described and defined in the Koran, the holy book of Islam. It is considered a religious duty to fight for

Islam when necessary. As part of the jihad, Saladin declared his intention to free the Holy Land from the Christian Crusaders.

Until now, the Crusaders had won every major battle in which their mounted knights had room to charge. The Christians' horses were much larger than those of the Muslims, and the Christians wore metal armor, whereas the Arabs and Turks wore cloth. Therefore, the Crusaders were confident as King Guy of Lusignan led the Christian army out of Jerusalem and toward Saladin's forces, which were drawn up near the banks of Lake Tiberias.

The Christians gathered water at a set of wells about ten miles (16 kilometers) from the lake, and rested for a few hours. An urgent war council was held. Many of the leaders wanted to return to Jerusalem because of the July heat and the lack of available water. Against their advice, King Guy and Reginald of Châtillon decided to march on. They had with them what they believed was the True Cross (the one on which Christ was crucified) and Crusader armies had never lost a battle in which they carried the relic. So the Christians advanced to their doom.

Saladin had prepared the way for them. As the Christians moved toward Lake Tiberias, they were harassed by countless attacks by Arab and Turkish horsemen. The Muslims did not carry long lances or wear heavy armor, but their light equipment gave them an advantage in the intense heat. The Crusaders plodded forward in a dogged fashion. Late that afternoon, they sighted the shimmering waters of Lake Tiberias, but Saladin and his army stood between them and the water. The Muslims then set fire to the dry grass around the Crusaders, creating blankets of thick smoke.

Saladin attacked the next day. He and his Muslim army won a great battle at the Horns of Hattin (where

Christ had preached the Sermon on the Mount) near the shores of Lake Tiberias, on July 4, 1187. Both King Guy and Count Reginald of Châtillon were taken prisoner in the battle. The two Christian leaders were brought to Saladin's tent.

Saladin offered King Guy a glass of water. Both Guy and Reginald knew that the Muslim sultan would not kill a man once he had offered him food or drink. Hoping to save Reginald's life, Guy offered his own water to Reginald. Furious, Saladin stepped in between the two men. He would not renege on his promise to spare Guy's life, but he offered Reginald a choice. Reginald had to make a choice, then and there, on the spot, to accept the Muslim faith or perish. Reginald refused to convert, and Saladin ran him through with his sword. The members of the Knights Templar and Knights Hospitallers who were captured during the Battle of Hattin met the same fate.

Saladin then proceeded to isolate Jerusalem by capturing a number of smaller Crusader cities, including Acre (pronounced *A-Kra*) and Sidon. He failed to take Tyre, which was defended by Conrad of Montferrat, one of the leading members of the Christian community in the Holy Land. Only by the middle of September was Saladin ready to try for the greatest prize of all: Jerusalem.

Saladin brought up his siege towers and was beginning to make progress when the city's inhabitants begged for mercy. A series of negotiations took place between Saladin and the city leaders. To everyone's surprise, Saladin agreed to spare the lives of the inhabitants and not to sack the city. He also offered to give those who could ransom themselves their freedom (the price was not cheap, however). The city leaders agreed, and on October 2, 1187, Saladin entered Jerusalem in triumph.

Saladin entered Jerusalem on October 2, 1187, according to the Christian calendar. To Muslims, it was the seventh day of Rajab in the year 583. The Muslim calendar began in the year 622, when Muhammad left Mecca for Medina. Regardless of which calendar one used, it was apparent that this was a momentous date: Saladin had recaptured Jerusalem from the Christians. Eighty-eight years of Christian rule had come to an abrupt end.

The Arab conquest was remarkably peaceful when compared to that of the Christian Crusaders of 1099. There were no massacres. Indeed, there was very little fighting at all. Saladin allowed a large majority of the population to be

The Three Holiest Cities of Islam

Mecca, Medina, and Jerusalem are the three cities that are holiest to Muslims. The first is the city of Muhammad's birth; the second is the place where he grew to become a leader; and the third is where he made a mystical night journey.

Born around A.D. 570, Muhammad was an orphan who was raised by an uncle and became a prosperous merchant trader. Not until about the age of 40 did he receive his first message from the Archangel Gabriel, who commanded him, "Recite the word of God!"

Muhammad's message—"There is no God but Allah and Muhammad is His Prophet"—was unpopular in his home city of Mecca. The people of Mecca worshipped a number of idols, the most important of which was a black meteorite that had fallen long before. In A.D. 622, Muhammad fled north to the city of Medina, where his teachings were welcomed. Muhammad fought a series of battles against his former townspeople, and in 632, he entered his home city in triumph. He smashed the idols that had long been worshipped there and established the Islamic faith, which has five pillars: a confession of faith (known as witness), prayer, fasting, giving alms to the poor, and a pilgrimage to Mecca at least once in a lifetime.

Muhammad died in 632, but the religion he started lived on. One of the articles of faith that developed after his death said that he had made a trip to Jerusalem at night, and from there, ascended to heaven. For these reasons, three cities, rather than one, are central to the Muslim faith.

ransomed; those who could not afford the ransom were sold as slaves.

Saladin became the foremost hero of the Muslim world. Mullahs (religious leaders), pilgrims, and spiritual seekers hastened to Jerusalem to offer their congratulations. Many of them hoped to be selected to deliver the first sermon at the Dome of the Rock, the place from which it was believed that Muhammad had ascended to heaven. Saladin selected 32-year-old Muhi ad-Din, "the reviver of religion."

Wearing a black robe that had been sent to him by the caliph (spiritual leader) of Baghdad, Muhi ad-Din told his audience that God, not their strength, had given them the victory over the Christians. Muhi ad-Din told the listeners

The Military Monks

The Crusades had an unexpected by-product: the establishment of several religious orders that were dedicated to fighting. In 1119, nine Christian knights in the Holy Land formed a monastic group called the Knights Templar because they guarded the temple in Jerusalem. The Templars were known for their white robes with red crosses, and their fierce dedication to the holy war against the Muslims.

Just one year later, in 1120, a number of Crusaders formed the Knights Hospitallers, also known as the Knights of the Hospital of St. John. They swore oaths of chastity, poverty, obedience, and protection of the Christians in the Holy Land.

The Knights Templar and Knights Hospitaller did not like one another, but between them they formed the core of Christian military strength in the Holy Land. Their defeat at the Battle of Hattin in 1187 came as a great shock to the Christian world.

In 1190, a handful of German knights formed the order that became known as the Teutonic Knights. This group established a hospital just outside Acre. The Teutonic Knights became known for their medical and charitable services, but they later became a major military order in northeast Germany, fighting the Russians and Poles.

to purify the city, which had been soiled by the presence of the Christian Crusaders, and to continue the struggle to bring the word of Allah to all parts of the world:

> Labor to expel the evil which afflicts us and tear up the enemy by the root; purify the rest of the land from this filth which hath angered God and his Apostle; lop off the branches of infidelity and cut through its roots; for now the times cry aloud: Vengeance for Islam! God is mighty! God conquers and subdues! He humbleth the infidel! [2]

It was a magnificent speech, equal to any that Pope Urban or Bernard of Clairvaux had given to launch the Crusades. With these words, Muhi ad-Din urged the continuation of the holy war against the Christians. Unknown to Muhi ad-Din or even to Saladin, however, the Christian Europeans were already making plans of their own—plans that would lead, in time, to the Third Crusade.

Two Kings and an Emperor:

Richard, Philip, and Frederick Barbarossa

This map shows the land and sea routes taken by Crusaders between 1096 and 1270. The arrows show the movements of Richard of England and Philip of France as they moved from southern France to Sicily, and then on to Cyprus and the Holy Land.

He is not dead, but seated beneath six knights at a table of stone, he sleeps in the Thuringian mountains, until the day when, at last, he will deliver Germany from slavery and make her leader of the whole world.

— German saying about Frederick Barbarossa

The news of Saladin's victory and the fall of Jerusalem reached Italy around the beginning of December 1187. Pope Urban III had just died; his successor, Gregory VIII, immediately began to preach what would become the Third Crusade. Gregory sent special couriers to the major European monarchs, asking them to set aside their usual quarrels with one another and to join together in a mighty crusade against the Muslims.

Even as he sent the messengers forth, Gregory knew that the chances of real cooperation were slim. The European monarchs had been at odds with each other—and with the papacy—for decades. Still, it was vital to make an attempt to present a united Christian European front in a new struggle for the Holy Land.

There were numerous princes in Europe in 1187. The three most powerful were the ones who received the papal message first: King Henry II of England, King Philip Augustus of France, and Frederick Barbarossa, the Holy Roman Emperor. Even the country names—England, France, and Holy Roman Empire—do not fully convey what Europe was like in 1187. England included the island nation of today, but Henry II also held significant lands in western France, and through his wife, Queen Eleanor, could claim the wine country of Aquitaine. Though he was king of England, Henry II spoke French better than he did English. The same was true of his wife and their seven children.

Philip Augustus was king of France, but he had nowhere near the power normally associated with that title. Philip had direct control of the Ile de France, the lands directly around Paris. His authority over the rest of France, though, was dependent on the good will of his counts, dukes, and knights. Many of these people did not like Philip; sometimes they were good and faithful subjects, and sometimes they were not. Philip's great ambition was to subdue his unruly noblemen and to conquer the lands that English King Henry II held in France. If he could achieve this, Philip would be considered the greatest French leader since Charlemagne, who had built a massive European empire that included all or parts of France, Germany, Italy, and Spain, among other places, in the eighth and ninth centuries.

This engraving of King Philip shows the monarch in later years. By then he had become King Philip Augustus ("the Revered One"). Philip's actions against the English and Germans allowed the Capetian monarchy to reclaim large areas of France, and made that country the greatest European power of the thirteenth century.

Frederick Barbarossa, who had taken the throne in 1152, had the most unwieldy title of all. Technically, he was Frederick, Holy Roman emperor of the German nation. The Holy Roman Empire corresponded roughly to what is Germany today, but at that time, it was hardly united at all. Frederick had about 200 counts, dukes, and local lords underneath him. In bad times, they often made the Holy Roman Empire completely ungovernable; in good times,

Frederick was able to impose his will on his subjects.

Henry of England and Philip of France were natural rivals. Frederick was less concerned with the French and the English. He had spent much of his reign trying to subdue the rebellious townspeople of northern Italy. Frederick had endured a terrible defeat at the hands of Swiss and Italian foot soldiers in the Battle of Legnano in 1177. Since then, Frederick had spent his time in Germany proper, and had given up his attempts to dominate northern Italy.

All three monarchs received the news of the Third Crusade at about the same time, either late in 1187 or early in 1188. All three swiftly agreed to put aside their disagreements and unite in a great crusade. One of the players, however, changed even before the crusading effort properly began. King Henry II of England died on July 6, 1189. His last words were, "Shame, shame on a conquered king."[3]

Henry had not been defeated by some far-off enemy but by the combined efforts of Philip Augustus and Henry's oldest surviving son, Prince Richard. Born in 1156, Richard had become one of the most aggressive and reckless of all European knights. He loved to make war, it seemed, and early in 1189, he joined Philip Augustus of France to fight against Henry. The old king died, and in September 1189, Richard took the throne as King Richard I. He was already known as Richard, *Coeur de Lione*, or Richard the Lionhearted.

Richard had conspired with Philip of France against his father for a number of reasons. First, Henry II had mistrusted his son, and had never directly declared that he wanted Richard to be his heir (in fact, Henry preferred his youngest son, Prince John). In addition, Henry was at odds with his wife, Queen Eleanor, of whom Richard was extremely fond.

Richard was crowned king of England in September 1189. All the Christian men who witnessed the coronation agreed that England had never had a more manly, vigorous, and chivalrous king. Women could not form an opinion, since they were banned from the ceremony. Jews, however, did form a quick impression of the new king, as a number of them were attacked by Richard's zealous servants. London's Jewish community did not recover from the attacks and the confiscation of its wealth for nearly a generation.

There was no doubt that Richard intended to go to the Holy Land on crusade and that he intended to bring Philip of France along with him. Although they had worked together in the past, Richard wanted to be sure that Philip would not attack or plunder any of Richard's possessions in France while he was gone.

Eleanor of Aquitaine

In an age that celebrated men and manly deeds, Eleanor of Aquitaine stands out as one of the best examples of what a woman could achieve in a man's world. In the 82 years of her life, she met popes, kings, and knights—and few were unimpressed by her.

Born in 1122, she was the daughter of Duke William of Aquitaine, in the wine country of southwestern France. Eleanor was married to King Louis VII of France, and the two went on the Second Crusade together in 1147. She bore him two daughters, but no sons, and the couple divorced in 1152.

Just weeks later, Eleanor married Henry of Anjou, who soon became King Henry II of England. Theirs was a passionate, stormy marriage. Together, they had seven children, five of them sons. The strong-willed Eleanor could not resist the lure of politics. Her husband eventually locked her up at the abbey of Fontevrault in France.

Eleanor was freed by her son Richard in 1189. He became king of England and was one of the leaders of the Third Crusade. Eleanor looked after Richard's interests in England during his absence. When Richard was seized and held prisoner by Germans, Eleanor raised the 100,000 marks of silver needed for his ransom. Richard returned safely home, and Eleanor retired to the abbey of Fontevrault, this time by choice. She died there in 1204, the best-known and most influential woman of the twelfth century.

Richard the Lionhearted was crowned at Westminster in 1189. Richard banned all women from the event. There were also persecutions of London's Jewish community that week.

Meanwhile, Emperor Frederick Barbarossa was making his own preparations. Born in 1125, Barbarossa was one of the oldest and most distinguished of all European monarchs. He was about 63 years old when the call for the Third Crusade came. Barbarossa might easily have sent one of his best generals or knights in his place. He had, after all, been to the Holy Land once already; he had served under his uncle Conrad III in the ill-fated Second Crusade of 1147–1149. The idea of staying home does not even seem to have occurred to Barbarossa, however. He had a reputation to maintain, as the most Christian and most warlike of the European monarchs. He was determined to go to the Holy Land a second time.

Barbarossa made careful plans. He wrote diplomatic letters to the king or prince of every country whose borders he would have to cross on his way to the Holy Land. These included the king of Hungary, the chieftain of Serbia, and the Byzantine emperor in Constantinople. Because Barbarossa had no fleet to speak of, he would have to travel by land, marching through the Balkans and Turkey, some of the most dangerous terrain known to Europeans of that time.

Sometime in May 1189, one month before the death of Henry II of England, Barbarossa gathered a great German army at Ratisbon (present-day Regensburg in southeastern Germany). Some historians believe he had a force of 100,000 men, but more careful analysis usually reduces that number to about 20,000. A great many of Barbarossa's soldiers were German knights, however, whose equipment was costly and whose warlike reputation was widespread. Even if there were only 20,000 troops, this was the largest and perhaps the most cohesive army Barbarossa had ever commanded. On May 11, 1190, the Germans moved out from Ratisbon.

All went well at first. The Germans crossed the Balkans safely and arrived at Constantinople. There, Barbarossa found that the Byzantine emperor was not eager to have such a large contingent of Germans linger in his realm. Some fighting took place between Germans and Byzantines before the two emperors came to an agreement. Barbarossa consented to leave Constantinople alone and march south to the straits called the Hellespont, where he and his men were ferried to the Asian side.

The Germans then made a slow and painful march across Asia Minor (Turkey). Not only were they harassed by Muslim raiders, but water was scarce, and many men died of thirst on the journey. In the spring of 1190, however, even before the French and English had started their own trip, Barbarossa passed through Armenia and was poised to enter Syria. He sent messages ahead to Saladin:

> Restore the land which you have seized! We give you a period of twelve months, after which you shall experience the fortune of war. . . . You, God willing, shall learn the might of our victorious eagles and shall experience the anger of Germany: the youth of the Danube [River] who know not how to flee, the towering Bavarian, the cunning Swabian, the fiery Burgundian, the nimble mountaineer of the Alps.[4]

Saladin replied by messenger that his men were too many to be counted, and that he could summon armies from as far away as Mesopotamia. Unlike Barbarossa, though, Saladin did not boast about the diversity of his men or the different climates from which they came. Virtually all of the Arab soldiers came from the hot desert areas of the Middle East.

On June 10, 1190, Barbarossa led the German army across the River Alph in Cilicia, now in southeast Turkey. It was a piercingly hot day, and the men were sweltering and irritable. So were their horses. In fact, Barbarossa was thrown from his horse halfway across the stream. Throughout his life, Frederick Barbarossa had survived at least a dozen battles, but this seasoned veteran did not die from a battle wound but by drowning after his fall from his horse.

Within a few days of his death, the Germans were a spent and broken force. Many went home. Many others were ambushed and killed in the mountains. Only a few thousand straggled forth and reached Acre, in the Holy Land, which was still in Christian hands.

Because of his attempts to unite the German nation, and because of his death while on crusade, Barbarossa became an important symbol to many Germans. They admired him almost as a mythological figure, as the English regard King

Frederick Barbarossa was in his sixties when the Third Crusade began. Never one to shrink from a task, he personally led the German army. Barbarossa died in a mountain stream as he neared the Holy Land.

Arthur. "He is not dead, but seated beneath six knights at a table of stone, he sleeps in the Thuringian mountains, until the day when, at last, he will deliver Germany from slavery and make her leader of the whole world."[5]

Without Barbarossa, the German element of the Third Crusade came to a swift demise. The crusade was now in the hands of the two other European leaders, Philip of France and Richard of England.

This painting of knights returning from a tournament is in the Musee Conde, in Chantilly, France. The red tunic with a striped cross on the man on the left indicates he may have been a member of one of the religious orders, such as the Knights Templar or Knights Hospitaller.

Richard and Philip:
Separate Paths to the Holy Land

If he does put her aside and marry another woman,
I will be the enemy of him and his so long as I shall live.

—King Philip of France, referring to Richard
the Lionhearted and Philip's sister, Alice

Richard was crowned king of England on September 3, 1189. He began massive preparations for the crusade almost at once. One policy that he found necessary to enact was a new tax. Swiftly called the "Saladin Tax," this levy took 10 percent of the income of every subject in the kingdom; only men who enlisted in the army were exempt from the special tax. Richard managed to force his subjects to comply, but King

Philip of France found his subjects in practical rebellion against the same type of tax; Philip repealed it.

The two monarchs were in close consultation with one another. Their former close relationship as conspirators against Henry II may have helped them achieve a type of cooperation that was seldom possible between England and France.

On June 24, 1190, which was the feast day of St. John the Baptist, Philip received the Oriflamme—a sacred banner that French kings used in medieval times—from Notre Dame. He was now fully invested with the power of the Catholic Church to undertake the crusade. Meanwhile, Richard and his army had crossed the English Channel. The two kings and their armies met at Vézelay, in north-central France, in early July.

Vézelay witnessed a spectacular show. The red banner of St. George, the English flag, flapped in the breeze alongside the blue and white fleur-de-lis of France. Knights jousted, servants hastened to support their lords, and Vézelay became the scene of one of the greatest meetings of medieval times.

Despite the celebrations, there was already some tension between the two monarchs. Philip made the situation awkward for Richard, insisting that Richard honor his long betrothal and marry Philip's sister, Alice. Richard avoided giving a straight statement on this point, and the two men threw small barbs at one another. Onlookers noticed that the English king consistently overshadowed the French monarch. In July, the two armies split ranks and marched off in separate columns: the French headed for Genoa, Italy, and the English headed to Marseille, France, both ports on the Mediterranean Sea. Unlike Frederick Barbarossa, who had drowned about one month earlier on his march overland, the English and French were going to the Holy Land by sea.

Richard expected to meet with an English fleet at Marseille. The fleet was delayed because its leaders had taken time out to help the king of Portugal with his war against the Moors (Arab invaders). Though this impeded Richard's progress, the fleet's generous gesture was remembered in Portugal for centuries, and became one of the reasons the two countries maintained a long friendship.

When the fleet did not appear, Richard chartered two ships and sailed on his own. He headed to Sicily,

Sicily in the Middle Ages

Sicily was grander and more politically important in medieval times than it is today. Sicily's position off the southern coast of Italy, and its close proximity to Africa, made it a natural meeting ground for Christians, Muslims, and Jews. For a century between about 1150 and 1250, Sicily boasted the best universities of Europe, and for a time, was the seat of government for Frederick II Hohenstauffen, the Holy Roman emperor.

The island already had a long and rich history that stretched back to the times when Carthage and Rome battled for power in the Mediterranean. Sicily, however, truly shone during the twelfth and thirteenth centuries, when a wealth of knowledge was transferred from the Arab Muslim world to Christian Europe.

Christian scholars were amazed that the writings of Aristotle, Galen, and Plato were more readily available in Arabic than they were in Latin. During the fifth and sixth centuries, when European literacy fell dramatically, Arabs brought precious manuscripts to Baghdad, where they were translated into Arabic. Now, in the High Middle Ages of the twelfth and thirteenth centuries, many translated versions of Greek and Roman scholarly works made their way back to Europe by way of Sicily and Spain, both of which were natural meeting grounds between Arab and European cultures.

Sicily continued to thrive as a place for learning for some time. Its position as a center of shipping, however, was eventually taken over by two powers on the Italian mainland: Venice and Genoa.

The leaders and knights of the Third Crusade went to the Holy Land by several routes. The scene at the top shows that Richard and Philip went by way of the Mediterranean Sea, whereas the men on horseback indicate the movement of Frederick Barbarossa and the Germans.

which was the rendezvous point for the two armies, but he took his time on the voyage. A number of times, he made the ships wait while he and a handful of courtiers rode horseback along the Italian coast, heedless of possible danger posed by pirates or brigands. Richard also met with an ambassador of the pope at Ostia in central Italy, but declined the Holy Father's invitation to come to Rome. Like many English monarchs of the Middle Ages, Richard believed that the papacy exerted too much power over the affairs of nations, and he did not wish to encourage any papal involvement in his crusade.

Philip arrived at Messina, Sicily, first. Richard came a few days later, and the two armies slowly converged, by sea, on the eastern end of Sicily.

The people of Messina, and of eastern Sicily as a whole, were not pleased when the English and French armies appeared. The residents of Palermo and Messina considered themselves some of the most educated and civilized people of their time and many of them looked down on the French and English soldiers. This led to tensions between the Crusaders and the townspeople.

Sicily was also going through a political crisis. Its king had died just a year earlier, and the throne was supposed to pass to a member of the Hohenstauffen family, of which Frederick Barbarossa had been the leader. The Sicilians had balked at the idea of a German king, however, and one of the Sicilian noblemen had crowned himself King Tancred.

Richard had been brother-in-law to the deceased king of Sicily; Richard's sister, Joan, was the king's widow. Richard made it clear that he wanted Joan to accompany him on the coming crusade, and that he favored King Tancred in the squabble over succession to the Sicilian throne.

Philip now took the opportunity to press his sister

Alice's claim to marry Richard. The English king put Philip off as long as he could, and tensions grew between the French and English soldiers, who were already agitated because of the difficult relations with the people of Messina.

Even if he ignored the conflicts between the Crusaders and the Sicilians, Richard soon had something else to cause him concern. His mother, the formidable Eleanor of Aquitaine, arrived by sea, bringing with her Berengaria, a Spanish princess from the kingdom of Navarre.

Eleanor was then about 69 years old. Very few medieval women would have undertaken the perilous journey from England to Sicily, and even fewer would have tried to force their will upon Richard the Lion-hearted. Eleanor knew her son, however. She knew that he was ambivalent toward marriage at best, and she feared that the royal family line would end with Richard. To try to prevent that from happening, she traveled from England to northern Spain, then brought Berengaria with her to Sicily.

Eleanor did not remain in Sicily for long. By the time she left, though, she had coaxed at least a verbal promise from Richard to marry Berengaria, and King Philip soon learned of it. Philip was furious, both for the honor of his sister Alice and for the damage that a marriage between Richard and Berengaria would do to the Franco-English alliance. The French king declared, "If he does put her [Alice] aside and marry another woman, I will be the enemy of him and his so long as I shall live."[6]

Despite such threats, Richard remained firm in his decision, and Philip had to back down. Richard agreed to pay some 10,000 pieces of gold to Philip to compensate for the dishonor he had brought to the French royal family.

By the time King Philip sailed from Sicily, in March 1191, the Franco-English alliance was strained. Philip made a swift crossing and arrived near the city of Acre, on the western border of the Holy Land, sometime in April. Richard's crossing soon after took an entirely different course.

Richard and Philip now knew the fate that had befallen Frederick Barbarossa. Both Philip and Richard were superstitious men, and they may have unconsciously sought ways to avoid danger in their own paths to the Holy Land. Richard now dawdled, taking his time on his voyage. He arrived at Rhodes, off the coast of Turkey, and was about to pass by Cyprus when he learned that the Byzantine ruler there had captured and imprisoned Crusaders who had been shipwrecked off the Cypriot coast.

The sensible thing would have been to bypass Cyprus and negotiate for the release of the prisoners sometime in the future. Richard, however, was irritated by the arrogance of the Byzantine ruler, Isaac Comnenus. Richard landed his troops on the southern coast of Cyprus and began a war against Comnenus. The English won two battles, not without some losses, and Comnenus quickly capitulated to Richard. In the celebrations that followed, though, Comnenus made a quick exit, and once again, made war on Richard. King Richard won the next confrontation as well, and had soon conquered most of the island. There was now no question of putting Comnenus back into power. The question was: Whom should Richard install as the new ruler? The English king made a poor choice: Guy of Lusignan, the former king of Jerusalem.

In the four years since his defeat at Hattin, Guy had not been an impressive leader. He had blundered in the defense of the city of Tyre, and the laurels there had gone to his rival, Conrad of Montferrat. Even so, Richard named Guy as the new king of Cyprus.

This relief shows Richard the Lionhearted in his favorite pose: heading into battle. Richard was a man of contradictions—brave yet cruel, chivalrous yet insensitive. Only on the battlefield did he live up to the words "beyond reproach."

The island of Cyprus also became the scene of the marriage of Richard and Berengaria of Navarre. The ceremony was held at Limassol, Cyprus, on Sunday, May 12, 1191, and was followed by huge celebrations.

The wedding concluded, Richard sailed at last for the Holy Land. He landed at the Christian lines around the city of Acre in the middle of June.

This idealized illustration shows Saladin in a moment of victory. Though he was often victorious, Saladin was more often the diplomat and man of words than the man of battle. Muslims today remember him for his magnanimous behavior and personal generosity, rather than his exploits in war.

The Siege of Acre

The Franks then flung themselves upon them all at once and massacred them with sword and lance in cold blood.

—Muslim account of the massacre of prisoners outside Acre

Acre was one of the largest and most important port cities of the Holy Land, which included, from north to south, Sidon, Tyre, Beirut, Acre, Jaffa, and Ascalon. In his victorious campaign of 1187, Saladin had come close to crushing all these cities, but had not done so. The southernmost ports—Jaffa and Ascalon—were in Muslim hands; the northernmost three—Sidon, Tyre, and Beirut—were held by Christians; and Acre, the city in the center, was now being besieged by the Christians. The siege had gone on for well over a year and it had drawn in the best resources of both sides.

The siege of Acre had been initiated by Conrad of Montferrat, the lord of Tyre. Conrad had done well in drawing a ring around the Muslim defenders, and Conrad's forces had been continually increasing in size because thousands upon thousands of volunteers who were arriving from Europe. The remnants of the German forces of Frederick Barbarossa had joined Conrad as well, and by the spring of 1191, the Christians were close to taking Acre.

Saladin now fought with a strong will to keep the resistance within Acre alive. Saladin and his army could not reach Acre to send reinforcements, but daring Muslim swimmers brought news of the siege and the outside world from one camp to another. Carrier pigeons were also used. Saladin knew that the cause of the people of Acre was desperate, and he was devastated to learn that Richard the Lionhearted had now landed to join the crusading army.

King Philip of France had arrived about six weeks earlier. Philip had not dallied in crossing the Mediterranean—and had Richard delayed his own crossing by just ten more days, Philip would most likely have received all the credit for the capture of Acre. This was because Philip had brought large siege engines—called mangonels—with him, and these machines began to hurl large stones at the walls of Acre.

Richard brought even more mangonels, and the two Christian kings enjoyed the sight of stones crashing into the walls of Acre. Within just days of his arrival, however, King Richard fell ill. Philip was suffering, too, and the two kings were left incapacitated. Their illness made all their hair fall out, and their alarmed physicians soon bled them to the point of weakness. Despite their physical state, both kings made a point of taking part in the military action. Richard and Philip had their servants bring them crossbows, with

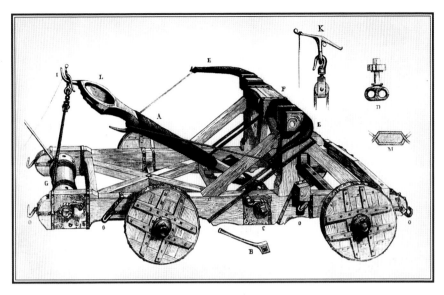

The mangonel was one of the highest developments of military technology during the Middle Ages. The throwing arm (A) hurled a stone from (L) that could fly 300 feet through the air and do great damage to a castle wall. The largest mangonel of the era was built by King Edward I of England. It was used against the Scots and was named, appropriately, "War Hammer."

which they fired shots at the Muslim forces. Numerous records state that Richard felled a number of Muslims, but given the distance and the position of his bed, this seems very unlikely.

The people of Acre resisted the Crusaders as best they could, but Richard found another way to destroy their will to fight. Richard promised a piece of gold to each member of the crusading army who would run up to the walls of Acre and pull a stone away from its foundation. Numerous men took the dare, and soon, Acre was on the verge of physical collapse.

The merchants and emirs of Acre sent as many swimmers with as many messages as they could to Saladin, asking him on what terms they should surrender. Saladin was despondent at the gravity of the situation; he knew the critical importance of this port city and did not wish to see its demise. Saladin sent word that the people of Acre should obtain the best terms possible and then yield to the Crusaders.

Negotiations began between the two Christian kings and the emirs of Acre. Richard and Philip understood the strength of their position, and they drove a hard bargain. Not only were the leading members of the city population to be ransomed for gold and silver, but Saladin was to deliver the True Cross, captured at the Battle of Hattin, to the Crusaders. All this had to take place within the next three months.

A swimmer brought the news to Saladin. The Muslim leader immediately rejected the terms, which he considered far too harsh. Just minutes later, though, Saladin's watchmen saw the Muslim flags come down all around Acre; they were soon replaced by the flags of England, Germany, and France. It was July 11, 1191, just over four years since Saladin's great victory at Hattin.

Richard and Philip entered the city in triumph the next day. Their entry was marred, however, by a disagreement between the English and German troops. The banner of Leopold, the duke of Austria, had been placed on many of the Muslim buildings. Seeing this, Richard's soldiers tore down the Austrian flag and ground it into the dust. The Austrian banner was replaced by Richard's personal standard; Richard did not want to share the glory with anyone. Not surprisingly, Duke Leopold and his Austrians departed the very next day. Leopold swore that he would get revenge for the way Richard had treated him.

Within days of their entry into Acre, Richard and Philip began to argue. King Philip announced that he had to return to France, both because he was sick and because he needed to tend to matters in his own country. Richard, too, had received messages urging him to come home; his younger brother, John, was interfering with the government of the

This illustration shows two things at once. The Crusader soldiers at the bottom left are taking the Muslim city of Acre, while King Philip and King Richard, at the center, are debating how to share the spoils. Philip soon pled illness and returned to France, leaving Richard as sole commander of the Third Crusade.

two regents Richard had left in control. Despite this concern, Richard was not about to turn back now, and he was initially furious that King Philip would choose to do so.

The angry discussions went on for several days. Finally Richard agreed that Philip could depart if he would swear not to attack Richard's holdings in France or those of any of Richard's allies, until the English king returned home. Philip made the vow and departed on a galley, headed for Italy.

Although he was furious over Philip's abandonment of the crusade, Richard was not displeased on the whole. He now was the undisputed master of all the Christian forces. Armed with the authority of that position, he pressed Saladin to deliver the ransom money and the True Cross, both of which had been promised in the surrender of Acre.

Saladin might simply have refused the terms of surrender, since he had not been there when they were made. Saladin, though, did his best to honor the agreement. He asked for an extension of three months in which to collect the money, but he was deliberately vague about the True Cross, which was no longer in his possession (he had long since sent it to Baghdad).

Days passed, and then weeks. In August, Richard's anger began to mount, and finally, he made a brusque and brutal decision. The 2,700 Muslim prisoners who had yet to be ransomed were led onto a field between the Christian and Muslim forces. A Muslim chronicler recounted what happened:

> In the afternoon of Tuesday, 27 Rajab [August 20, 1191] about four o'clock, he came out on horseback with all the Frankish army, knights, footmen, Turcoples [cavalrymen dressed in eastern style and carrying a bow and lance], and advanced to the pits at the foot of the hill of Al 'Ayadiyeh, to which place he had already sent on his tents. The Franks, on reaching the middle of the plain that stretches between this hill and that of Keisan, close to which place the sultan's advanced guard had drawn back, ordered all the Muslim prisoners, whose martyrdom God had decreed for this day, to be brought before him. They numbered more than three thousand and were all bound with ropes. The Franks then flung themselves upon them all at once and massacred them with sword and lance in cold blood.[7]

Seeing this, the Muslim army made an immediate attack, but it was too late. The Crusaders killed all the prisoners and still managed to fend off the assault. The next day, the Crusaders retired to the walls of Acre, and the Muslims came in to find and bury their dead. They found that the Christians had slit the throats and bellies of many of the prisoners, hoping to find gold or jewels that the men might have swallowed. The Muslims were enraged, and Saladin vowed that any Christians who fell into his hands would receive a swift death.

King Richard never gave an explanation or apology for his actions that day. As one of his biographers commented, "The murder of his Muslim prisoners at Acre reveals the worst side of Richard's character; he could not endure being thwarted and when he was opposed strongly enough to frustrate his designs, there was no depth to which he would not sink in order to relieve his frustration."[8] This was certainly the lowest point of a crusade that had already been marred by international rivalry between the Christian princes.

Arsuf and Al-Adil

This illustration depicts men from Saladin's army. The illustrations on their shields show their lineage and ethnic loyalties. Saladin was a master at combining men from Egypt, Syria, and Mesopotamia. Even more than the Crusader force, his army was a mixture of ethnic and tribal groups.

Al-Adil should wed the king's sister, whom he had brought with him from Sicily at his crossing over. . . . She was to be established at Jerusalem and her brother would yield her all the places he held in the Sahel.

—Proposal from King Richard to Saladin, carried by Saladin's brother, al-Adil

Richard led his army down the coast. As the Crusaders advanced due south, they found small Muslim forces to their left, making constant harassing attacks. King Richard disdained to respond to the attacks; he ordered his men to continue their march in close formation, and not to waste their energy defending against the Muslim harassment.

Both the Templars who led the vanguard, and the Hospitallers who brought up the rear, were vexed by this order. The knights were eager to chase the Muslims and inflict casualties upon them. Despite the knights' disappointment, Richard's orders were kept until the army reached the vicinity of Arsuf, where Saladin had arranged for the whole of his army to prevent any further movement by the Crusaders.

Saladin was under increasing pressure from his emirs. The Muslim nobles had brought their retainers and peasants to the holy war, but Saladin was not acting like the victorious general he had been just four years ago. He was reacting to what the Christians did, rather than dictating to them.

In truth, Saladin was not the same man he had been in 1187. The passage of four years had aged him greatly. The sultan was about 53, but he had been increasingly worn down by the strain of the campaigns, the fatigue caused by long marches, and the fear that his reconquest of Jerusalem might be undone by this fearsome Crusader, Richard the Lionhearted. Saladin would probably have chosen to keep shadowing the Crusaders, harassing them in their march, but he yielded to the pressure of his emirs and prepared for battle.

King Richard seems to have known a battle was coming. As the Christian force emerged from the forest between Acre and Arsuf, Richard laid his battle plans. He knew that the Muslims still had a great superiority in numbers, and he also knew that the Crusaders were less accustomed to fighting in the deadly heat than their Muslim opponents were. Therefore, Richard commanded that the army hold its position exactly in column formation; no deviations were permitted until the king gave the order. Showing his foresight, Richard had the packhorses and wagon trains moved to the side closest to the coast. He arranged his army in two lines: the first composed of infantry and the second of mounted knights. He made sure that the headstrong Knights Templar and Knights Hospitallers knew that they must remain in formation until he gave the order to charge.

The difference between a Christian mounted knight's heavy and awkward metal armor and the lighter protective gear of a Turkish or Arab mounted warrior was illustrated in this quotation from an Arab document:

> The armament [of the Turks and Arabs] consists of a hard, durable armor, not too heavy and not too light, of a helmet with a connected cap under the helmet. . . . The equipment for combat consists of two strong bows, thirty arrows with straight, pointed tips, a hard middle piece, and iron wings, in a medium-sized quiver.[9]

The Battle of Arsuf began at around ten in the morning, on September 7, 1191. Saladin's thousands of lightly armed Turkish horsemen began a series of charges against the infantry line on Richard's left flank. The Turks were really more like mounted bowmen then true cavalry; they moved in swarms rather than formations, and they used every opportunity to unleash a rain of arrows upon their foe.

Saladin's Turks made significant headway against the Christian infantry, but the heavy armor of the Christians protected them from most of the arrows. At no point were the Turks able to penetrate the line of armored Christian knights. For their part, the Christians steadily became exhausted as morning turned into early afternoon. The sunlight and heat were unrelenting, and their heavier armor and equipment, though advantageous in so many ways, weighed the Christians down.

The Crusader knight, on the right, has been wounded by an arrow. The Muslim warrior, on the left, has accomplished his goal. Throughout the two centuries of Crusader warfare, the Muslims were more lightly armed and armored than were the Europeans. Sometimes this was an advantage; sometimes not.

The Knights Templar, bringing up the Christian rear, suffered the most from the Turkish attacks. Three times, the Templars' leaders sent messages to Richard, begging him to allow them to launch a cavalry attack. Each time, the answer returned in the negative. Richard was determined to have Saladin bring all his resources into the battle and commit all of his troops. Then, when it was obvious that the entire Muslim army was engaged, Richard himself would lead the deadly charge of the knights.

That was the plan—and if not for the exhaustion caused by the heat and the state of near-madness caused by the thousands of falling arrows, the plan might have worked. Sometime around two in the afternoon, though, the Knights Templar could stand the condition no more. Two or three of their leaders, in a state of heat exhaustion and perhaps near-delirium, made a reckless charge on their own. The other Knights Templar followed, mistakenly believing that the order for a general engagement had been given.

Any charge by Christian knights was frightening. The massive horses, bred over generations in Western Europe, carried large men wielding lances, axes, and swords. Whenever lightly armored Muslim cavalrymen encountered Christian knights in the open field, the Muslims had to give way. The Muslims, however, were adept at falling back, dispersing, and then suddenly regrouping when the moment seemed right. By doing so, they could attack the Christian knights at the moment that those massive horses were winded from exertion and pick off the Christian soldiers at their leisure.

Richard knew the danger well, and he was no King Guy of Jerusalem, ready to be lured into a trap by Saladin. Seeing that the Knights Templar had disregarded his orders and started their charge, Richard went straight to join them. The Muslims and Turks began to give way all along the line.

Saladin was furious at this turn of events. He rode close to the line of battle and shouted encouragement to his men, but it was too late. The Christian knights had brushed aside the first line of Muslim resistance, and the battle threatened to become a catastrophe for Saladin and the Muslim cause.

Perhaps it was heat and sunstroke that prevented the Christians from winning an overwhelming victory at Arsuf. When the day was over, the Christians counted nearly 7,000 fallen Muslims, but the success might have been much greater if the mounted knights had been able to pursue. Instead, the sun went down on one of the largest Christian victories in a generation, and on the confirmation of Richard as one of the great warrior-leaders of his time.

The Battle of Arsuf also came near to destroying the reputation of Saladin. Like King Richard, Saladin was not a despot; he needed the support of his emirs as much as Richard needed that of the leading noblemen. Saladin had built a reputation for invincibility in the aftermath of the Battle of Hattin in 1187. That reputation now disappeared. Saladin, who knew better than anyone how fortunate he had been to win so many victories in the past, now turned increasingly to prayer. He begged Allah to help him find a way out of the situation.

Saladin was not blind to the possibilities of negotiation. He knew that King Philip had left and was probably now back home in France. Saladin knew that Philip might attack some of Richard's properties in France, and Saladin had already commenced a series of secret negotiations with Conrad of Montferrat, who was back in the city of Tyre. The negotiations that now opened between Richard and Saladin were the most surprising of the entire Third Crusade.

Soon after he first reached the Holy Land, King Richard had sent emissaries to Saladin, asking for a conference. Saladin had refused, stating that kings and princes should not meet until the details of the disagreements between them had been worked out. Now Richard appealed to Saladin once again, and he made the Muslim leader quite an offer.

Saladin's younger brother, al-Adil, carried messages between the two leaders. Most of the Christians who met al-Adil thought him a comely and gallant man; some expressed sorrow that such a man of distinction was

Richard the Lionhearted, shown in the thick of battle at Arsuf. It is no exaggeration to say that Richard was one of the most fearless and skillful of all the knights of the Middle Ages.

fighting for the opposing cause. Around October 20, 1191, just six weeks after the Battle of Arsuf, Richard sent al-Adil to Saladin with a proposal.

> Its substance was as follows: That Al Adil should wed the king's sister [Joan], whom he had brought from Sicily at his crossing over; for her husband, the king of Sicily was then dead. She was to be established in Jerusalem and her brother would yield her all the places he held in the Sahel—to wit, Acre, Jaffa, Ascalon, and their dependances. The Sultan, on his side, was to give Al Adil all that he possessed in the Sahel and declare him king of that country. Al Adil was to retain all the towns and the fiefs he actually owned; but the Holy Cross was to be restored to the Franks. The villages were to be given up to the Templars and Hospitallers, while the strongholds were to be reserved for the newly-married pair.[10]

This offer was intended to settle everything. Saladin and Richard would each withdraw from the area, leaving the Holy Land for the new couple to rule.

Al-Adil brought the proposal to his brother Saladin. All chroniclers agree that Saladin showed a surprising willingness to accept the proposition and agreed to the terms on the spot. Whether he was really pleased with the deal or was play-acting is difficult to determine, but Saladin had probably gathered that Richard was not serious about his offer. When al-Adil rode back to the Christian camp and announced that Saladin had agreed, Richard hesitated, saying that Joan had flown into a rage when he told her she had to marry a Muslim. The agreement could still go forward, Richard said, but al-Adil would have to convert to Christianity. This demand effectively put an end to the negotiations.

Toward the end of October, Richard led the Crusader army out of its quarters at Jaffa. As had been true at Acre, the soldiers were reluctant to leave; they enjoyed the wine, women, and music of the coastal city. Now they had to march over barren desert land to their goal: Jerusalem.

It would be interesting to know how many, or how few, in the Crusader army really knew what Jerusalem was like. Not many of them were survivors from the army of King Guy of Jerusalem, but there must have been some such men to tell tales. Jerusalem came to have many meanings for the thousands of soldiers: French, English, and German alike.

For his part, Saladin knew very well what Jerusalem was like, and he despaired of defending it against this formidable enemy. Saladin had tried his best to prevent the Crusaders from taking Acre; and he had fought them in the open terrain at Arsuf. Now he had grave doubts as to whether he could defend Jerusalem. Briefly, he considered abandoning the holy city. Saladin was dissuaded from this by his emirs, who reminded him that the average Muslim soldier who had been recruited for the jihad would not accept the loss of the holy city to the Christians. Why had they fought and died, if not to protect the sanctuary where Muhammad had commenced his trip to heaven?

As they advanced, most Crusader soldiers knew little of the conspiracies and intrigues that surrounded their enterprise. They may have thought it was a straightforward matter of capturing Jerusalem, but they knew little about how Saladin, Richard, and Conrad of Montferrat negotiated and dealt with complicated offers and counteroffers. Behind all the maneuvers and countermaneuvers, there was real desperation. Both Richard and Saladin were actually near the end of their tether. Saladin's reputation as the great warrior of Islam had suffered mightily in the past six

Here, Richard the Lionhearted is seen as a lawgiver and dispenser of justice, as well as a warrior with great dedication, indicated by the battle axe. During his ten-year reign (1189–1199), Richard spent only six months in England. The rest of his time was spent on the Third Crusade and fighting for his lands in Aquitaine.

months, and he feared some of his emirs might desert him. Richard's reputation had soared during that same period, but Richard did not appear to know how to make the most of the situation. Though he was a great warrior and a skillful general, Richard seems to have been a very poor strategist. Jerusalem was only 40 miles (64 kilometers) away, but Richard blundered back and forth in the hills and valleys of the Holy Land, unable to make up his mind to make a march on the city. Richard the Lionhearted was one of the greatest battlefield improvisers ever to live, but he could not design a strategy and hold to it. Instead, he dithered on the march to Jerusalem.

This illustration depicts the culmination of one of the many sieges of Jerusalem. It shows a vision of Jerusalem as beautiful, holy, and worthy of all the sacrifices that were required to win it. The painting hangs in the Biblioteca Capitolare in Padua, Italy.

So Near and Yet So Far

As an unworthy Crusader, he shielded his eyes and shrank away from the glare, as if gazing upon Jerusalem without capturing it were a disgrace and a sin.

—Historian James Reston, Jr., describing Richard the Lionhearted as he viewed Jerusalem from a distance

During the winter of 1191–1192, Richard had come close to Jerusalem. He turned around and returned to Jaffa, however, because he did not think he could capture the holy city in winter.

Richard soon left Jaffa as well. He and a large body of troops marched south, directly along the coastline, to Ascalon. This had once been a large and beautiful city, but Saladin had destroyed it the previous summer, lest it suffer the same fate as Acre. Richard now had his men begin to rebuild what had been ruined.

In April, Richard returned to Acre, where he held a major conference with his leading barons and knights. The time had come, Richard said, to decide who would be king of Jerusalem once the city was retaken: Would it be Guy of Lusignan, who had lost the city in 1187, or should it be Conrad of Montferrat, who still governed the city of Tyre?

There was no question as to which man Richard preferred. He had always shown a marked preference for Guy. Even so, the barons and knights chose Conrad by a vote that was nearly unanimous. Richard may have been furious, but if so, he disguised his displeasure and accepted Conrad's nomination. News was quickly sent to Tyre, where Conrad prepared for his coronation as the new king of Jerusalem.

Events soon changed the situation dramatically. In the spring of 1192, Conrad of Montferrat was assassinated in the streets of Tyre by two men from the Isma'lis, Order of the Assassins. Montferrat's death threw the delicate politics of the Middle East into considerable confusion. Because he had always backed King Guy of Jerusalem against Conrad, King Richard was immediately suspected of having hired the Order of the Assassins to remove his great rival. This is unlikely, but Richard continued to be linked to Conrad's assassination for three years.

Conrad's death helped neither Richard nor Saladin. The latter was desperately trying to organize the defenses of Jerusalem, and had come to the sad conclusion that a successful defense was impossible. Not only would the city eventually fall to Richard's siege engines, but the great

Muslim army would be captured, too. Saladin was on the verge of emptying the holy city and leaving it to the Christian invaders.

During the late winter and early spring of 1192, Richard and the Christian army came close to Jerusalem on two occasions. One of these moments was described

The Assassins

The very word *assassin* comes from words that mean "hashish-eater." There is no mistake in the correlation between the terms: One led to the other.

Sometime around 1090, the leader of a radical sect of Islam founded his order, called the Isma'lis, among a group of mountain fortresses in northern Persia and eastern Syria. The leader became known as the Old Man of the Mountain, famous for his fanatical beliefs and his ability to persuade his converts to carry out assassinations.

Hashish was involved. The Old Man lured young men into drug-induced states, then persuaded them that they had had a temporary glimpse of heaven. That vision could become permanent, if they were willing to obey the Old Man's every command. So it was that hundreds, even thousands, of young men became killers.

The Isma'lis were universally feared. Saladin was nearly killed by them once, and afterward, he maintained a lifelong dread of their stealth. Conrad of Montferrat was assassinated by them in Tyre, even as he was about to celebrate his being named king of Jerusalem. Later, there were also threats against the lives of European monarchs, including Edward I, better known as Edward Longshanks, due to his great height and stature.

Neither Crusader campaigns nor Muslim armies were able to quell the Isma'lis. They thrived until about 1258, when a large Mongol army led by a brother of Kublai Khan broke down their mountain fortresses and brought the killing cult to an end. The Isma'lis did not disappear, however; their more peaceful descendants survive today as one of the branches of Islam.

by both contemporary chroniclers and by more recent historians:

> On a narrow ridge they caught a few more unlucky Arabs. Richard knocked one from his horse, and then, as he withdrew his Excalibur from the chest of his victim, he raised his gaze and saw in the distance . . . Jerusalem!
>
> The sight was a surprise and a shock. It tormented rather than gladdened him. Its proximity, a mere three miles away, was sheer torture, for it was so beautiful and so elusive and perhaps unattainable. His longing was almost unbearable. The city was like the holy flame and he the lowly moth, and his wings were singed by the heat. As an unworthy Crusader, he shielded his eyes and shrank away from the glare, as if gazing upon Jerusalem without capturing it were a disgrace and a sin.[11]

This was the closest Richard would ever come to his goal. Like Moses, who had been permitted a view of the land of Israel but was not allowed to enter it, King Richard the Lionhearted would never enter the holy city.

That same month, Richard learned of a rich caravan of trade goods making its way from Egypt to Jerusalem. Rather than allow one of his lieutenants to carry out the capture, Richard himself led a night attack on the caravan. He and his men made off with a great deal of silver and gold, as well as wine and women. The episode showed Richard at his most daring and reckless: a magnificent military leader, with too little concern for his own life or the ultimate success of his mission.

Saladin now despaired of ever defending Jerusalem. Still, when he learned that the Christians had attacked the trade caravan and made off with most of its contents,

This woodcut illustration shows Jerusalem, the city that is holy to three faiths. From the time that Pope Urban II first called Jerusalem the "nave [center] of the world," until the end of the Crusades, this was the final destination and goal of the Crusader armies.

Saladin vowed that the Crusaders would not have such an easy a time taking Jerusalem. He took the step of poisoning the wells for a ten-mile (16-kilometer) radius around the holy city.

Though it was severe, the tactic was hardly unheard-of. The Turks had poisoned those same wells 90 years earlier when the troops of the First Crusade had besieged Jerusalem. The poisoning had not stopped the Christian leaders then, and there was no reason to think it would stop Richard the Lionhearted now.

Something had disheartened the mighty warrior, though. As the fervor of his men increased, Richard's own enthusiasm seemed to subside. The most painful and humiliating moment for Richard came in late June, as the Christian army came within ten miles (16 kilometers) of the holy city. He had just returned from the successful pillage of the caravan. Rather than command the army forward, Richard assembled his barons and delivered the following words:

> Wherever our army goes, Saladin knows our plan, the course we plan to follow, the number of our force. We are far distant from the coast. If he should move around our flank and take his army into the Ramla plain and block the passage of our provisions, it would be disastrous to our besiegers. They would pay and pay dearly. Moreover, the perimeter of Jerusalem is long, and its walls are thick and strong. It would take a great number of our soldiers to breach these walls. Who then would protect our supply lines? No one. These supply trains would be destroyed one and all, if there were no one to relieve them.[12]

The barons could hardly believe their ears. Was this Richard the Lionhearted, who had led them from France to Sicily, from Sicily to Cyprus, and from Cyprus to Acre? Was this the warrior who had won the battles of Acre and Arsuf? They could not understand why he now cowered at the thought of danger, whether to the besiegers or to the supply trains. Some of the barons urged Richard to put aside his fears and begin the march to Jerusalem.

Remarkably, Richard refused. He offered, instead, to resign his command and fight under the authority of any leader the barons chose to name. Richard would fight and die with the rest, but he would not willingly lead his men into what he believed would be a death trap. The king did not get his wish.

The conference broke up. Richard remained the Crusader commander-in-chief, but he was a leader without a will. The crusade had stopped just a short distance from its ultimate goal. For his part, Saladin could hardly believe his good fortune. He had never expected mighty Richard the Lionhearted to give up when he was so close to taking the holy city.

The Peace
of Saladin

The knight lifts his sword and urges his mount forward. The combined force of a charging horse and the blows struck by a mounted man were enough to terrify many opponents. The knight on horseback dominated European battlefields from about 1100 to 1350. Only the advent of the crossbow and longbow allowed men on foot to have a real chance to defeat the mounted knights.

The sultan had finally emerged victorious in his arduous confrontation with the West.

—Amin Maalouf, *The Crusades Through Arab Eyes*

Victory was now within Saladin's grasp. For Richard, too, there would be one last scene of romance and glory. About one month after Richard refused to lead his men in the final push, the Christian army retraced its steps to the coastal city of Jaffa. The Crusader soldiers were not unhappy to enjoy the pleasures that could be found in Jaffa, but they were still disconcerted by Richard's recent turnaround.

Saladin knew that the passage of time worked in his favor.

His spies informed him that Richard was deluged with requests to return to England and take care of affairs in that kingdom. Saladin may have guessed that Richard had lost his nerve or his heart for the final conquest. In any event, Saladin now wanted to punish the Crusaders, to persuade them never again to threaten Muslim control of the Holy Land.

Saladin led his army out of the vicinity of Jerusalem and headed toward Jaffa. It is not certain whether Saladin knew it, but Richard was not there; he had sailed north to Acre, and so was not at Jaffa to defend the city against Saladin's approach.

Saladin's army laid siege to Jaffa. The Crusader forces there were smaller in number than any Christian army the Muslims had yet encountered. After a siege of three days, the Crusaders' defenses were penetrated. Not all of the city fell at once, but Saladin was in control of at least two-thirds of Jaffa when King Richard's war galley was spotted in the distance.

Learning of Saladin's advance, Richard had crammed three ships full of men and sailed south from Acre. This was a pitifully small force with which to resist the size of Saladin's army, but Richard was determined to make a stand. As he sailed into the harbor of Jaffa, Richard saw a great array of Muslims drawn up on the beach to hold him back. Beyond those men were thousands of others spread throughout the city.

Only one fortress remained in Christian hands, and its defenders raised their flag to show the king they were still free. The sight of that flag inspired Richard even more than he had been before. All the chroniclers agree that Richard jumped off his war galley even before it landed on sand, crying out, "The Devil take the hindmost!"

Inspired by the sight, Richard's men followed him.

Instead of being checked or overwhelmed on the beach, the Christians surged forward. Within half an hour, they had cleared the beach of Muslims; after three hours had passed, they had retaken the entire city of Jaffa. This was one of the most remarkable military events of the Third Crusade, perhaps of all the Crusades put together.

Saladin was not in the city when Richard's forces retook it. He and his emirs were camped perhaps two miles (three kilometers) outside the walls. They heard the din and saw the smoke, but knew little until they saw the Muslim crescent banners descend and the banners of England and France replace them.

Saladin was both astonished and mortified. He knew the importance of morale in any army, and his force, collected for the purpose of jihad, was especially vulnerable to a possible loss of enthusiasm. Therefore, Saladin sent his best cavalrymen forward to battle for the outskirts of Jaffa against the Christian foe.

No major battle was fought that day, but one week later, there was a major confrontation between Christian and Muslim knights near Jaffa. There were times when it appeared that the Muslims with their superior numbers would defeat the Crusader army, but each time, King Richard appeared to make the difference. It was said that, at one point, he rode out before the entire Muslim line of knights and not one came out to oppose him in single combat, so great was his reputation and fame at that moment.

Saladin taunted his men who returned from the fight: "Where are those who are bringing me Melek Richard as my prisoner? Who was the first man to seize him? Where is he, I say, and why is he not brought before me?"

The Muslim knights answered: "Know, O king, for a surety that this Melek of whom you enquire is not like other men. In all time no such soldier has been seen or heard of: no warrior so stout, so valiant, and so skilled. In every engagement he is first to attack and last in retreat. Truly we tried hard to capture him but all in vain; for no one can bear the brunt of his sword unharmed; his onset is terrible; it is death to encounter him; his deeds are more than human."[13]

This day marked the summit of Richard's military reputation, but it was also the end of the Third Crusade. Richard showed no more aptitude than before for leading

Maimonides

Whether they were in Europe or the Holy Land, most Jews found the Crusades to be a nuisance at best, and a terror at worst (there were massacres of European Jews before the First Crusade). During this time, however, the greatest figure of medieval Jewry lived and thrived—Maimonides.

Born in Cordova, the capital of Muslim Spain, Maimonides moved to Egypt in his youth. He trained at the best schools and became one of the leading physicians of his day. During the twelfth and thirteenth centuries, the hospitals of Cairo, Damascus, and Baghdad were far superior to those of London, Paris, or Vienna. Maimonides eventually became the personal physician to the new vizier of Egypt, none other than Saladin himself.

For most of the rest of his years, Maimonides had a difficult life, traveling constantly to serve the medical needs of Saladin and his family, while also continuing his own medical research. So great was Maimonides's reputation, that a few years after Saladin's death, Richard the Lionhearted sent messengers all the way to Egypt to ask Maimonides to travel to England and become his personal physician. Maimonides did not comply.

Aside from being a doctor and medical researcher, Maimonides was also a philosopher. He knew the Old and New Testaments, the Torah and the Talmud, as well as the Koran. He wrote a number of books, the best known of which is *Guide for the Perplexed*, which came out in 1190. The *Guide* shows Maimonides to be a deep, thoughtful philosopher, for whom the rigors of science and the mental exercises of religion were equally important.

his men to Jerusalem, and if they did not do that, there was little reason to stay in the Holy Land. Richard was plagued by news of what was happening back home in his kingdom. He was also sick. He was ready to bring his crusade to a close, so he opened negotiations with Saladin.

The sultan was chastened by what had happened at Jaffa. He saw that he would not be able to chase the Christians away with force; he would have to entice them to leave. As had happened before, Saladin's brother

Maimonides was one of the most important Jewish intellectual and scientific leaders of his day. Born in Spain, he trained at the best schools and later became personal physician to Saladin in Egypt.

Maimonides died in 1206. His body was taken from Egypt to Palestine, where his tomb remains today. Maimonides's life shows just how much a talented and dedicated person could achieve in medieval times. For many Jews, Maimonides is the most important leader of the Middle Ages.

al-Adil carried a series of messages back and forth from the Christian and Muslim lines.

Saladin announced that he would allow Christian pilgrims of all social ranks to visit Jerusalem in peace. Richard accepted that offer with pleasure, but wanted to keep the fortress-city of Ascalon, located 20 miles (32 kilometers) south of Jaffa, as well. Saladin was adamant on this point. He had begun his jihad in response to Reginald of Châtillon's attacks on Muslim caravans, and he wanted no fortress that would allow such activity to happen again. Saladin did not ask to control Ascalon himself. Instead, he demanded that it be dismantled stone by stone, and that neither side should fortify it in the future.

Richard finally yielded on the issue of Ascalon. Al-Adil continued to serve as messenger until the two rulers were ready to make peace. It was not a peace intended to last for all time, but rather a five-year truce between Christians and Muslims in the Holy Land. Under its provisions, the Christians would keep all the coastal cities they now held, from Sidon and Tyre in the north to Acre and Jaffa in the south. Ascalon would be dismantled, and Saladin would allow—even welcome—Christian pilgrims to Jerusalem. Control of the holy city would remain with the Muslims, however. This was the single most important condition as far as Saladin was concerned. Anything less than the retention of Jerusalem would have risked the reputation and fame he had earned through the jihad of 1187.

On September 2, 1192, the terms of the truce agreement were brought to Richard. The English king was sick and weak with fever. As the Muslims offered to read aloud the entire document one last time, Richard waved to silence them. It was enough, he said; he knew the terms and agreed to them. The Third Crusade was over.

Saladin returned to Jerusalem and then to Damascus. He was weary and worn, having gone through the jihad and the Third Crusade without the services of his favorite physician, Maimonides of Egypt. Saladin had become the greatest hero the Arab and Turkish world had seen in more than 100 years. He had surpassed Zengi and Nur ad-Din, both of whom had been great warrior kings, but neither of whom had ever developed a reputation for modesty, generosity, or mercy, as had Saladin.

This painting shows a weary Crusader, returning after years of fighting and toil. This knight, at least, makes a peaceful return. King Richard the Lionhearted was taken captive by Henry VI, Holy Roman Emperor, and kept in prison until an immense ransom was paid.

Richard's Odyssey

Friends I have many, and promises abound;
Shame will be theirs; if for winters twain,
Unransom'd, I still bear a tyrant's chain

—Poetry written by Richard the
Lionhearted when he was in captivity

The crusade was over. It was time to go home. Richard was among the last to leave, departing from Acre in October 1192. He set out in a war galley, accompanied by about 40 of his men. Richard did not expect that any of his fellow Christians would consider working against him. After all, he had just led Europeans in one of the most gallant—if unsuccessful—causes. Then again,

Richard had never counted his costs very carefully, and he had failed to realize just how many enemies he had made over the past several years.

When he had departed from England in July 1190, Richard had left the kingdom in the hands of his brother John and his mother, Eleanor. John had quickly worked to undo many of Richard's programs, and had formed a partnership with Philip of France, who had arrived home toward the end of 1191. Between them, Prince John and King Philip were carving up Richard's wealthy Aquitainian inheritance in France. John and Philip were not Richard's worst enemies, however. His most virulent foes were German.

During a brief squabble with King Tancred of Sicily before leaving for the Holy Land, Richard had dishonored some of his German allies. Worse, when Acre fell, Richard had ruled that his flag alone should fly over the captured city (the flag of the duke of Austria was torn down and stamped on by English troops). This insult had, naturally, caused the duke and many Austrians to leave the crusade, and they had long memories.

There was also one more motivation to harm Richard. Through the amazing feats of arms and valor he had performed in the Holy Land, Richard had become known as the greatest knight of the Christian world. If he were seized and held for ransom, there was almost no limit to how much ransom his captors could demand. Envy, national pride, and simple greed all conspired to win Richard far more enemies among his fellow Europeans than he might have expected.

Richard found everything aligned against him as he set off on his trip home. First, his ship was blown around the island of Cyprus for weeks. Then, he was blown off course nearly as far as Marseille, France, where he did not wish to land: Philip's power was too strong there. Finally, Richard settled on landing on the west coast of Greece.

It may seem strange that Richard did not simply sail out the Straits of Gibraltar and head home to England. It was November and December, however, which threatened bad weather. Shipping techniques were also not as advanced as they would be a century or two later; the compass had not even been invented yet. Had Richard sailed due west and possibly been shipwrecked off the coast of Muslim Spain, his fate might have been terrible.

As it happened, Richard's trip hardly went as he had planned. Richard and his small party proceeded up the Dalmatian coast and entered the domain of the duke of Austria. Knowing the enmity that the duke held for him, Richard tried to hide his identity with a number of disguises. None of these lasted very long; Richard was simply too striking in appearance to pass for anything but a knight or lord. Finally he was caught at an inn just outside of Vienna. Richard made one last attempt to disguise himself, this time as a cook, but he was apprehended and taken to prison.

The duke of Austria rejoiced. He held the arrogant Richard the Lionhearted as a prisoner—but not for long.

Henry VI had become Holy Roman emperor after the death of Frederick Barbarossa. Henry now sent word that he wanted Richard, and that he would pay a huge sum to get him. The duke of Austria acceded to his lord's demand, and Richard was transferred from Vienna to Ratisbon for a payment of 60,000 pieces of silver.

Christian Europeans hardly knew what to think of the matter. Although many of them believed that Richard was, indeed, an arrogant man who deserved to be humbled, they worried about the kind of precedent that would be set if a king were sold by a duke to an emperor.

Richard was brought before the emperor at Ratisbon. Henry delivered a long speech in which he accused Richard of having slighted and belittled the Germans during the crusade. The old rumors that Richard had hired the Isma'lis

Henry VI was the German leader who held Richard the Lionhearted in captivity. Henry had nothing against Richard; he wanted the ransom money so that he could pursue his dynastic interests, which included reconquering the island of Sicily.

to kill Conrad of Montferrat resurfaced. The situation looked ominous for the king of England.

Richard, however, responded to Henry with eloquence and even some charm. He praised the former emperor,

Barbarossa, and applauded the German effort in the crusade. He denied the accusation about Montferrat's death and asked leave to write to the leader of the Isma'lis, the "Old Man of the Mountain," to prove his innocence. Finally, Richard accused his younger brother, John, and King Philip of France of spreading evil rumors about him. He pointed out that those two men stood to gain a great deal: They were pulling Richard's lands apart while he was being held in captivity.

It was a fine speech. When Richard concluded, he seemed to have won the heart of the emperor. Henry seemed delighted with Richard and his manly refutation of the charges against him. Richard was soon dressed in much finer garb, given better meals, and sometimes even allowed to accompany the emperor on walks. There was no talk of freeing Richard, however. He was too valuable for that.

Henry VI had a special reason to keep Richard, a reason connected to the politics of the Holy Roman Empire. Henry's wife, Constance, was heir to the Norman kingdom of Sicily, which had been usurped by Tancred of Lecce during Richard's time there. Henry wanted very much to make Sicily part of the Holy Roman Empire, and he believed that he could obtain enough money from Richard's ransom to finance a military campaign there. Then, too, Richard was a brother-in-law to Henry the Lion, duke of Saxony, who led the opposition to Henry VI within the Holy Roman Empire. For these reasons, Henry VI was inflexible in regard to Richard's ransom; the emperor set his demand at the gargantuan sum of 100,000 marks of silver. Although the expression "a king's ransom" had existed prior to 1193, it was the circumstances of Richard's captivity that made the term a part of every-day speech.

Richard could only wait and see what happened. He

fell into melancholy at certain periods, and sometimes he composed lines of poetry to describe his predicament:

> Yet to the sad 'tis comfort to complain
> Friends I have many, and promises abound;
> Shame will be theirs; if for winters twain,
> Unransom'd, I still bear a tyrant's chain.
> Full well they knew, my lords and nobles all,
> In England, Normandy, Gascony, and Poitou
> N'er did I slight my poorest vassal's call;
> All whom money could buy from chains withdrew.[14]

Something did occur to raise Richard's spirits. The Old Man of the Mountain sent a letter to the kings and queens of Europe:

> The Old Man of the Mountain to Leopold, Duke of Austria, greeting. Whereas several kings and princes beyond the sea have accused our lord Richard, King of the English, of the murder of the marquis [Conrad of Montferrat], I swear by the God who reigns eternally, and by the law which we observe, that no blame attaches to him in regard to the death of that noble. . . . Be assured that we do not kill any man in this way for the sake of reward or for money, but only when he has first inflicted an injury on us.[15]

Apparently, Conrad of Montferrat had harmed the Isma'lis by stealing a ship from them. In any event, the letter meant that Richard was no longer accountable for Conrad's death.

When the ransom demand was forwarded to England, Prince John naturally refused to pay. It was impossible and it would ruin the kingdom, he said. Some of the English barons, however, pointed out that the kingdom was already in a very poor state of affairs and that it was imperative for John to do something quickly. Still, John hesitated. He was forced to do his duty only by his mother, the irrepressible Eleanor of Aquitaine.

Eleanor had seen her once-beloved husband turn against her and even imprison her. She had seen him die, felled by his son's intrigues against him. She had seen the elaborate preparations for the Third Crusade and Richard's dramatic departure, and she had had the fortitude to convince Richard to marry Berengaria of Navarre. Now, Eleanor learned, the crusade had failed, and Richard was being held by the Germans.

Eleanor leaped into action. Then in her mid-seventies, she orchestrated the raising of Richard's ransom. She attended fairs, flattered and threatened lords in turn, and begged the merchants of London to contribute. The money she collected never seemed to be enough, until finally, in early January 1194, Eleanor had raised the 100,000 marks of silver she needed.

On February 4, 1194, Emperor Henry VI released Richard into the custody of his mother. The ransom had been paid. Richard was free to return home.

Historians have ever since pondered whether 100,000 marks was too much to pay, even for the celebrated warrior-king. The mere possession of 100,000 marks of silver should have been enough for Germany to assert itself as the greatest power of the day. Emperor Henry VI was, in fact, able to campaign in southern Italy, and in 1194, he was crowned king of Sicily. He died just over two years later, though, and in the long run, his Sicilian policy was less useful to the history of Germany than it was to the ambitions of his family, the Hohenstauffens.

Richard returned home swiftly. His galley reached English soil on March 12. There was some scattered resistance to Richard's return, the most concentrated part of which came from the shire of Nottingham. Richard defeated the rebels with the help of some local outlaws led by a romantic rebel named Robin Hood, giving rise to the legend that has persisted ever since.

Just two months later, Richard left England and sailed to his lands in France. On May 28, he received the formal submission of his brother John. According to tradition, the older brother met the younger with the words, "Think no more of it, John. You are only a child who has had evil counselors."

Richard accepted John back into good graces, and John put aside his treacherous thoughts—but only for the moment.

Robin Hood

How much truth is contained in the many tales of Robin Hood, Friar Tuck, and Maid Marion? Rather little, most scholars say, and yet the persistence of the stories does give at least some information about English society.

During the reign of King Henry II, England had changed from a land of local government to one with centralized rule. Henry had been a supreme monarchist, intent on expanding his royal rights. Sheriffs, bailiffs, and town councils were now expected to serve the king.

All this centralization went against Anglo-Saxon tradition. People such as Robin Hood resisted the law, both to keep away greedy taxmen and to assert their rights as freeborn Englishmen. Most Robin Hood stories depict King Richard as a kind, benevolent monarch, and Prince John as a wicked man. The stories conveniently forget that it was Richard who had instituted the special Saladin Tax in 1189, and that Richard's ransom cost England more than all of John's follies combined.

Robin Hood and his band of thieves do illustrate something that lies deep within Anglo-Saxon custom, though. The English people have a distinct sense of fair play, and if they believe the government is extorting money from them, then it is their duty to steal from the rich and give to the poor. Whether or not there was an actual Robin Hood concealed in Sherwood Forest, the idea of Robin Hood certainly demonstrates the attitudes of English subjects in Richard's day—and beyond.

The stories of Robin Hood and his band of thieves date from the time of the Third Crusade. While Richard the Lionhearted spent only six months of his reign in England, his younger brother John oppressed peasants like Robin Hood, who used Sherwood Forest and other wooded areas to escape the arm of the law. Such men as Robin Hood considered King Richard the best of men, and his brother John the very worst.

Although the fighting against the Muslims had concluded in September 1192, Richard's putting down the revolt in Nottingham and forcing John to submit to his power can be seen as the last acts in the long drama of the Third Crusade. Richard was back in his lands, but he would not remain there for long.

The abbey of Fontevrault in western France holds the crypts (tombs) of King Henry II, Queen Eleanor, and King Richard the Lionhearted. The husband, wife, and son repose peacefully in death, but they were seldom at peace in life. Richard was always Eleanor's favorite child, but he and his father, Henry II, feuded bitterly.

The Contenders Pass

I forgive you my death.

—Richard the Lionhearted to the crossbowman who killed him

Richard was still in confinement in Germany when his old foe Saladin died of natural causes in Damascus on March 4, 1193, at the age of 55. Those who were with Saladin in his last days testified to his world-weariness and his readiness to depart. Saladin left a set of instructions for his son ez-Zaher:

> My son, I commend thee to the most high God. . . . Do His will, for that way lies peace. Abstain from shedding blood . . . for blood that is spilt never sleeps. Seek to win the hearts of the

people, and watch over their prosperity; for it is to secure their happiness that thou art appointed by God and me. Try to gain the hearts of thy ministers, nobles, and emirs. If I have become great it is because I have won men's hearts by kindness and gentleness.[16]

Another account of Saladin's character comes from an Arab account that described his attitude toward money:

His treasurers, Baha al-Din reveals, always kept a certain sum hidden away for emergencies, for they knew that if the master learned of the existence of this reserve, he would spend it immediately. In spite of this precaution, when the sultan died the state treasury contained no more than an ingot of Tyre gold and forty-seven dirhams of silver.[17]

Saladin's splendid funeral was followed by a great emptiness among the people of Damascus. Would there ever be another Saladin? Would the people find another ruler who was so gentle, gracious, and forbearing? The answer was no. Saladin's son lacked his father's talent for government. Egypt, Syria, and Palestine remained united under Muslim rule, but Saladin's passing marked the end of the best times for the dynasty.

The person who benefited most from Saladin's death was his younger brother, al-Adil, who followed a long tradition of usurpation in the Arab world; seldom did sons succeed peacefully to their fathers' thrones. It was not a surprise when al-Adil took power for himself.

Al-Adil did not have Saladin's charm or charisma, but he was an excellent administrator. Under his rule, the three kingdoms of Arab Syria, Arab Jerusalem, and Arab Egypt held together. Al-Adil was not troubled by the presence of the Christians in the port cities they had retained from the

Third Crusade; he believed it made better sense to trade with them than to fight them.

Relations in the region continued in this way for many years. In 1218, however, the Christian soldiers of the Fifth Crusade attacked both the Kingdom of Jerusalem and Egypt. At that time, al-Adil died of a heart attack. The Ayyubid Dynasty, founded by Saladin, continued to hold power for another generation or so, but there was no future Saladin among the family's members.

Meanwhile, in Christian Europe, King Richard began to fight King Philip again almost as soon as he returned to his Anglo-French estates. The two men feuded year after year over lands in Normandy, Anjou, and Aquitaine. Most of the stories that have come down to us of these battles testify to Richard's strength and will, but his victories were often ephemeral. King Philip was slowly drawing a noose around English lands in western France. The French king was waiting for a perfect moment to force out the English altogether.

It took some time for that moment to arise. Richard the Lionhearted provided it through his rash courage. In 1199, Richard besieged the castle of Chalus in southern France, where some impertinent barons had refused to pay Richard the annual tribute. It was a small campaign that Richard should have assigned to any one of his men, but he insisted on conducting the siege himself. As Richard rode around the castle one day, a crossbowman named Peter Basil shot a bolt that wounded Richard deeply in the arm. Richard ordered an immediate assault, and the castle was taken.

By then, however, it was clear that the king's wound was mortal. Richard ordered that all the defenders be killed, save the crossbowman, who was brought before him. The king demanded to know what wrong he had ever done to Peter Basil. The crossbowman replied that the king had killed Basil's father and two brothers in the course of his military campaigns. Basil said, "There, take any revenge on me that you want, for I will endure the greatest torments you can devise, so long as you have met with your end. For you have inflicted many and great evils on the world."

For once, Richard had truly met his match in bravery. The king finally said, "I forgive you my death."[18] He also commanded that Peter Basil be released and given 100 English shillings.

Richard died on April 6, 1199. He left his body to the abbey of Fontevrault, where his father was buried. He left his kingdom to his younger brother, John.

Richard was gone. In his decade on the throne, he had spent only six months in England. Most of the time had been on crusade or in France. Still, England claimed him as its own, and the world's most magnificent statue of Richard stands outside the Parliament buildings in London.

Now, after Richard's death, came Philip's perfect moment. Philip had endured pain and humiliation at the hands of both King Henry II and Richard the Lionhearted. At last, Philip had an opponent whom he could both out-maneuver and outfight: King John.

Philip won some of the English barons to his cause through bribes. Others eventually joined him because of their disgust with King John. By the spring of 1204, Philip had chased the English entirely out of Normandy and Anjou, and was poised to strike at Aquitaine. In that same year, Eleanor of Aquitaine, the formidable duchess and queen who had been wife to two kings and mother to two more, died at the abbey of Fontevrault. She was buried in the same place as Henry II and Richard the Lionhearted. This was a sad time for the people of England, who remembered the greatness of the royal family and the English empire. King John would soon bring even worse times to his people.

In 1209, John quarreled with Pope Innocent III. The pope placed all of England under interdict, meaning that none of the sacred rites of the Catholic Church, including communion and confession, could be performed. One year of this punishment brought the English people close to revolt. To appease them, John made peace with Pope Innocent III. In the document of submission, John agreed to state that he was a vassal of the pope, and that he held all of England only by the pope's consent.

Soon after this humiliation, King Philip struck again. In 1214, John and Otto IV, the Holy Roman emperor, went to war against Philip of France. It seemed as if the two great powers of England and Germany, located on two different sides, should have been able to easily squash France between them. Instead, Philip defeated the Anglo-German army completely at the Battle of Bouvines. Otto IV lost his throne, and John seemed close to losing his as well.

Rather than give up everything, John signed an agreement with his barons in June 1215. Known as Magna Carta (The Great Charter), the document has ever since been considered one of the cornerstones of English liberties. Although the Magna Carta primarily protects the rights of the barons and the Church—not ordinary people— from the king, the document was still of great importance in the development of the Anglo-Saxon concept of freedom from tyranny. The people of the Western world owe this great document to the cast of characters involved in the Third Crusade: Henry II, whose attempts to centralize England provoked resistance; Richard the Lionhearted, who spent so much time away from England and on crusade that the government lost even more of its appeal; and Eleanor of Aquitaine, who, in her desire to free her son, emptied the pockets of the English subjects. Most of all, the Magna Carta came about thanks to John, who, in his unsuccessful wars with the French and his conflict

Magna Carta (The Great Charter) was signed by King John in 1215. John, who was the favorite son of King Henry II, had brought the kingdom low. He had feuded with Pope Innocent III, who placed all of England under interdict— this was a censure that withdrew the sacraments and the right to Christian burial from all those living in England. John also lost the last English land possessions in France to King Philip. John signed the Magna Carta in June 1215 and it has remained a cornerstone of English liberties ever since.

with Pope Innocent III, brought the English realm to its lowest point.

John died of natural causes in 1216. His rival, Philip of France, died in 1223. Philip left France a much stronger nation than he had found it. Because of his tireless work against the English royal family, France expanded twofold during his reign, and for the rest of the thirteenth century, it was the richest and most powerful of the European nations. Saladin had been the first of the fighters of the Third Crusade to die; Philip was the last.

The Third Crusade holds a unique place in the history of the Christian West and the Muslim Middle East. No other crusade, earlier or later, pitted two kings and an emperor against a sultan. Even these mighty royal figures could not achieve success, though. With Barbarossa's death, the German contribution to the crusade diminished greatly. Then, Richard and Philip were unable to cooperate, which prevented any possibility of their winning Jerusalem together.

Despite Richard's battlefield heroism, Saladin must be acknowledged both as the greatest figure of the crusade and as its winner. Saladin may not have been as personally powerful or as inspiring as Richard, but he showed— throughout the war—a greatness of spirit that was unmatched. Time and again, Saladin might have collapsed under the strain of his efforts; instead, he remained strong, and in the end, he saved Jerusalem for Islam.

Although Saladin won the war and the Muslims kept Jerusalem, the English, French, and Germans achieved something of their own. They discovered the valor of their leaders and soldiers, and learned as well that valor alone was not enough to win wars. The Christian Europeans would have to find a way to cooperate if they ever hoped to win back the Holy Land.

1095	Pope Urban II gives speech at Clermont, France.
1096	The Peasants' Crusade, led by Peter the Hermit, fails.
1097	The Knights' Crusade begins.
1098	Siege of Antioch on the Orontes.
1099	Crusaders capture Jerusalem.
1137	Saladin born in Mesopotamia (what is now Iraq).
1146	Zengi takes Edessa.
1147	Bernard of Clairvaux gives speech for the Second Crusade.
1147–1149	The Second Crusade.
1152	Eleanor of Aquitaine and King Louis VII divorce; Eleanor quickly marries Henry Plantagenet.
1154	Henry II and Eleanor become king and queen of England.
1157	Richard the Lionhearted is born.
1164	John, the youngest child of Henry and Eleanor, is born.
1171	Saladin becomes the vizier of Egypt.
1174	Nur ad-Din dies; Saladin becomes leader of both Egypt and Syria.
1185	King Baldwin of Jerusalem dies; Guy of Lusignan is chosen to succeed him.
1187	Saladin declares a jihad against the Crusader states; he wins the Battle of Hattin and captures Jerusalem.
1188	Both Henry II and King Philip of France vow to go on crusade.
1189	Henry II dies; he is succeeded by his son Richard the Lionhearted; Frederick Barbarossa leaves Germany on crusade.
1190	Richard and Philip leave France on crusade; they spend the winter in Messina, Sicily; Frederick Barbarossa drowns in eastern Turkey.
1191	
March	Philip leaves for Acre.
May	Richard leaves for Acre.
May	Richard marries Berengaria of Navarre in Cyprus.
June	Richard arrives at Acre.
July	Acre surrenders to the Crusaders.
August	Philip leaves for home; Richard kills 2,700 Muslim prisoners.
September	Richard wins the Battle of Arsuf.
Autumn	Saladin destroys Ascalon; negotiations take place between the two leaders.

1192

April	Conrad of Montferrat is chosen to be the new king of Jerusalem; he is assassinated that same month.
June	Richard comes within three miles (five kilometers) of Jerusalem.
July	Richard withdraws to Jaffa and then Acre.
August	Battles of Jaffa.
September	A five-year truce is made.
October	Richard leaves the Holy Land.
Autumn	Saladin returns to Damascus; Richard taken prisoner in Austria.

1193

March	Saladin dies in Damascus.

1194

March	Richard ransomed for 100,000 marks of silver.
1195	By this year, al-Adil had become the leader of Saladin's dynasty.
1199	Richard dies from a wound inflicted by a crossbow; John becomes king of England.
1204	Eleanor of Aquitaine dies at the abbey of Fontevrault; she is buried there, beside her husband, Henry II, and her son Richard.
1209	Pope Innocent III places England under interdict.
1214	King John and his German allies lose the Battle of Bouvines to Philip of France.
1215	King John is forced by his barons to sign the Magna Carta.
1216	King John dies.
1218	Al-Adil dies.
1223	Philip dies.

CHAPTER 1: THE FIRST CRUSADE

1. W. Michael Blumenthal, "The Invisible Wall," *BusinessWeek online*, *http://www.businessweek.com/ chapter/blumenthal.htm*, 1998, accessed December 9, 2002.

CHAPTER 2: THE SECOND CRUSADE AND THE *JIHAD* OF 1187

2. James Reston, Jr., *Warriors of God: Richard the Lionheart and Saladin in the Third Crusade*. New York: Anchor Books, 2001, p. 91.

CHAPTER 3: TWO KINGS AND AN EMPEROR

3. Michael Farquhar, "Wicked Family Feuds," *Discovery Online*, *http://www.discovery.com/ stories/history/royal/part4.html*, 1998, accessed December 9, 2002.
4. James Reston, Jr., *Warriors of God: Richard the Lionheart and Saladin in the Third Crusade*. New York: Anchor Books, 2001, p. 128.
5. Marcel Pacaut, *Frederick Barbarossa*. New York: Charles Scribner's Sons, 1970, p. 208.

CHAPTER 4: RICHARD AND PHILIP

6. James Reston, Jr., *Warriors of God: Richard the Lionheart and Saladin in the Third Crusade*. New York: Anchor Books, 2001, p. 149.

CHAPTER 5: THE SIEGE OF ACRE

7. T. A. Archer, *The Crusade of Richard I*. New York: G. P. Putnam's Sons, 1889, p. 130.
8. James A. Brundage, *Richard Lion Heart: A Biography*. New York: Charles Scribner's Sons, 1974, p. 135.

CHAPTER 6: ARSUF AND AL-ADIL

9. Hans Delbruck, *Medieval Warfare, The Art of War*, vol. III. Lincoln, NE: University of Nebraska Press, 1990, p. 209.
10. T. A. Archer, *The Crusade of Richard I*. New York: G. P. Putnam's Sons, 1889, p. 188.

CHAPTER 7: SO NEAR AND YET SO FAR

11. James Reston, Jr., *Warriors of God: Richard the Lionheart and Saladin in the Third Crusade*. New York: Anchor Books, 2001, p. 303.
12. Ibid., p. 309.

CHAPTER 8: THE PEACE OF SALADIN

13. T. A. Archer, *The Crusade of Richard I*. New York: G. P. Putnam's Sons, 1889, p. 312.

CHAPTER 9: RICHARD'S ODYSSEY

14. James Reston, Jr., *Warriors of God: Richard the Lionheart and Saladin in the Third Crusade*. New York: Anchor Books, 2001, pp. 369–370.
15. Ibid., p. 372.

CHAPTER 10: THE CONTENDERS PASS

16. Will Durant, *The Age of Faith: A History of Medieval Civilization—Christian, Islamic, and Judaic—from Constantine to Dante: A.D. 325–1300*. New York: Simon and Schuster, 1950, p. 602.
17. Amin Maalouf, *The Crusades Through Arab Eyes*, trans. Jon Rothschild. New York: Schocken Books, 1985, p. 179.
18. James Reston, Jr., *Warriors of God: Richard the Lionheart and Saladin in the Third Crusade*. New York: Anchor Books, 2001, p. 382.

Archer, T. A., ed., *The Crusade of Richard I*. New York: G. P. Putnam's Sons, 1889.

Armstrong, Karen, *Islam: A Short History*. New York: Modern Library, 2000.

Bradbury, Jim, *Philip Augustus, King of France 1180–1223*. New York: Longman, 1998.

Brundage, James A., *Richard Lion Heart: A Biography*. New York: Charles Scribner's Sons, 1974.

Delbruck, Hans, *Medieval Warfare, The Art of War*, vol. III. Lincoln, NE: University of Nebraska Press, 1990.

Durant, Will, *The Age of Faith: A History of Medieval Civilization—Christian, Islamic, and Judaic—from Constantine to Dante: A.D. 325–1300*. New York: Simon and Schuster, 1950.

Gillingham, John, *The Life and Times of Richard I*. London: Weidenfeld and Nicolson, 1973.

Lamb, Harold, *The Crusades*. New York: Doubleday, 1930.

Maalouf, Amin, *The Crusades Through Arab Eyes*, trans. Jon Rothschild. New York: Schocken Books, 1985.

Pacaut, Marcel, *Frederick Barbarossa*, trans. A. J. Pomerans. New York: Charles Scribner's Sons, 1970.

Reston, James Jr., *Warriors of God: Richard the Lionheart and Saladin in the Third Crusade*. New York: Doubleday, 2001.

Samuel Willard Crompton teaches both Western civilization and American history at Holyoke Community College in Massachusetts. He lives in the Berkshire Hills, which are known for their scenery and pastoral surroundings. He is the author or editor of more than 20 books, with titles ranging from *100 Military Leaders Who Shaped World History* to *Meet the Khan: Western Views of Kuyuk, Mongke, and Kublai*. He is also a major contributor to the *American National Biography*, a 24-volume compendium issued by Oxford University Press.

Caspar W. Weinberger was the fifteenth secretary of defense, serving under President Ronald Reagan from 1981 to 1987. Born in California in 1917, he fought in the Pacific during World War II then went on to pursue a law career. He became an active member of the California Republican Party and was named the party's chairman in 1962. Over the next decade, Weinberger held several federal government offices, including chairman of the Federal Trade Commission and secretary of health, education, and welfare. Ronald Reagan appointed him to be secretary of defense in 1981. He became one of the most respected secretaries of defense in history and served longer than any previous secretary except for Robert McNamara (who served 1961–1968). Today, Weinberger is chairman of the influential *Forbes* magazine.